Foreword

Reform of local government has been on the political agenda for 25 years, although real progress in meaningful change has been limited to date. It is now time for action.

My objective is to create a modern, efficient and properly resourced local government system. This Programme charts a course for local government into the new millennium. It is based on ambitious goals which, with the whole hearted support of councillors and staff, are achievable. It offers local government an opportunity to re-establish itself as the legitimate voice of local communities and to lead government action in support of those communities.

I am now inviting local authorities to work in partnership with me to instil a new sense of purpose and pride in our local government system.

Brendan Howlin T.D.
Minister for the Environment

Minister's Foreword

Contents

Part One

Contents

1

Contents

2

Chapter 7 - ORGANISATIONAL ISSUES   65

SUMMARY OF KEY ACTIONS   75

Part Two

LOCAL GOVERNMENT SERVICES   81

APPENDICES

MAPS

Contents

3

Acronyms

AMAI	Association of Municipal Authorities of Ireland
CEB	County Enterprise Board
CEG	Community and Enterprise Group (3.10)
DOE	Department of the Environment
ENFO	Environmental Information Service
EPA	Environmental Protection Agency
EU	European Union
FÁS	Foras Áiseanna Saothair - The Employment and Training Authority
GCCC	General Council of County Councils
GDP	Gross Domestic Product
IT	Information Technology
LAC	Local Appointments Commission
LGMSB	Local Government Management Services Board (6.10)
MEP	Member of the European Parliament
NESC	National Economic and Social Council
NGO	Non Governmental Organisations
NRA	National Roads Authority
OECD	Organisation for Economic Co-operation and Development
OPLURD	Operational Programme for Local Urban and Rural Development 1994-1999
PCP	Public Capital Programme
RSG	Rate Support Grant
SMI	Strategic Management Initiative
SPC	Strategic Policy Committee (2.19)
UDC	Urban District Council
VEC	Vocational Education Committee
VFM	Value for Money

Part One

Chapter 1 **Introduction**

Local government services and achievements

1.1   The local government system and the services it delivers play a crucial role in the economic and social life of the State. In terms of economic activity, it accounts for the spending of almost IR£2 billion per annum, approaching five per cent of GDP. It raises taxation of some IR£340 million and provides employment for nearly 30,000 people throughout the country. Local government provides an extensive range of essential infrastructure, social and community services and is the part of our democratic system closest to the citizen.

1.2   The achievements of local government can all too easily be taken for granted. Local authorities have over the years provided 300,000 homes for people otherwise unable at the time to house themselves; 100,000 of those homes are still under local authority administration accommodating about 350,000 people, and the accommodation needs of some 10,000 households are being met every year through the various social housing schemes in which local authorities are the key agencies. A substantial programme to improve facilities in the existing stock of council houses and apartments has been under way for some time. And the local authorities have assisted many thousands to enter the private housing market over the years through grants and loans.

1.3   There has been considerable progress by local authorities in extending a piped supply of good quality water to most homes in the country. At present, ninety eight per cent of homes have a piped supply, most of which is provided either directly by local authorities or through support for private or group schemes. In their role as planning authorities, local authorities are responsible for shaping our towns and countryside through the provision of infrastructure to facilitate development, through framework plans for development, and through development control procedures. Bearing in mind the rapid development of the past forty years, local authorities have been largely successful in their planning functions notwithstanding well publicised difficulties in one or two local areas about land zonings. In recent times there have been substantial improvements in our cities, towns and villages under urban renewal schemes in which local authorities have played a significant role.

1.4   Local authorities have also been the main architects of our rapidly improving road network, currently being upgraded to European standards. They maintain some 96,000 kilometres of roads, ranging from new sections of motorways to cul-de-sac by-roads in isolated rural areas.

1.5   Local authorities have a critical role to play in protecting and maintaining the high quality of our environment. They are the main agents in developing our water and waste water infrastructure to meet stringent national and EU requirements. They have a continuing role in the generation of strategic plans for waste disposal, and for air and water quality and in implementing those plans through licensing the vast majority of discharges to the environment. They also have extensive public safety functions, including protection from fire - both preventive and through operating the fire brigades - and promotion of water safety and road safety.

1.6 Local authorities are the major providers of recreation and amenity infrastructure. Their library services ensure access to a valuable educational tool even in the smallest communities. The quality of many local authority public parks is widely acknowledged. And local authorities provide extensive facilities for sports such as football, tennis, swimming, and pitch and putt.

Weaknesses

1.7 Local authorities therefore play a significant role in the economic and social life of the country and have a record of achievement of which they can justifiably be proud. However, there are factors which inhibit the optimum functioning of the system -

- By international standards, the range of functions of Irish local authorities is narrow. Local authorities have no role in policing, public transport or personal social services and very little in health or education. They are not therefore in a position to offer a comprehensive response to problems confronting local communities - for example, traffic or drug abuse. This causes communities to look to central Government to solve their problems, or to propose new arrangements locally.

- Since the abolition of rates on domestic property and land, the system has been inhibited by a shortage of resources and an over-dependence on central Government decisions which are made annually as part of the budgetary process. The most obvious example of this constraint on resources was the deterioration in the condition of the non-national roads network prior to the initiation of the new restoration programme in 1995. But it is also manifested in the reduced funding allocated to the maintenance of other local facilities and in the inability of local authorities to take on even relatively small capital projects without special outside funds. Local authorities have also found it difficult to respond with financial support to worthwhile community initiatives.

- Through lack of resources and inability to respond to problems which transcend their traditional functions, local authorities have tended to be by-passed by the growth of new forms of community development organisations, many of which are attracting State and EU support.

- Day-to-day pressures arising from the wide range of essential public services for which they are responsible can mean that councillors and senior management are diverted from the broader, longer-term issues concerning the future role of the local authority and the direction it should take. The urgent may crowd out the important. Change is required to ensure that councillors and senior management can give more attention to planning for the future, while at the same time addressing the need for satisfactory arrangements to deal with operational matters.

- Excessive central control of many activities of local authorities - particularly in the staffing area - has tended to stifle initiative and to encourage referral of problems to central Government.

- The small scale of local authority operations has made it difficult for them to employ personnel with the expertise necessary to cope with increasingly complex environmental issues.

- The policy role envisaged for councillors has not been fully realised because, as part-timers, they have found it difficult to fulfil this role in the absence of well developed support systems. The system as a whole can therefore lean more in favour of the permanent officials.

Improvements in recent years

1.8   Since 1990, a number of significant reforms have been introduced. These have included:

- the establishment of three new county councils in Dublin to ensure a greater focus on local needs and priorities;

- the establishment of eight regional authorities to promote the co-ordination of public services in each region and to advise on the implementation of EU funding programmes;

- the introduction of broad powers of general competence for local authorities to act in the interests of the local community - relaxing substantially the archaic 'ultra vires' rule;

- the removal of a large range of statutory and administrative controls in areas such as local authority personnel, land disposals, traffic management, etc;

- the provision of broad powers for the making of bye-laws to regulate a variety of local matters;

- the introduction of a seven-year term of office for local authority managers in line with practice for heads of government departments;

- the establishment of the Environmental Protection Agency (EPA) and the National Roads Authority (NRA) to support and assist local authority environmental protection and national roads services, respectively; and

- the introduction of new rules for local elected office designed to limit the extent of the dual mandate.

Time for a strategic approach

1.9   It is now time to build on the reforms of recent years by the adoption of a strategic approach to the renewal of local government. This must take as its starting point the commitment by the Government in its policy agreement, *A Government of Renewal*, to

> the reform of our institutions at national and local level to provide service,
> accountability, transparency and freedom of information. In so doing, we are committed
> to extending the opportunities for democratic participation by citizens in all aspects
> of public life.

A programme for change

1.10 There are some key issues of public policy decided by central Government to which local authorities - all public bodies, for that matter - must have regard. Equally, there are factors outside the control of the individual local authority which inhibit the development of the local government system. This is where this Programme fits in.

It is designed:

- to outline public policy issues which the Government wishes local authorities to address as part of their strategic management process; and

- to identify factors which inhibit effectiveness and to set out a plan of action designed to improve the situation, an agenda to which public policy will work and which will achieve positive results.

1.11 The Government is working to achieve change through the Strategic Management Initiative (SMI), a multi-faceted programme for reform and renewal of the public service as a whole. However, if public service renewal is to be real and lasting it must also come to a significant extent from within organisations themselves: there must be self-renewal. This renewal process is already under way in local authorities. As part of the SMI, local authorities were asked by DOE in March 1996 to develop strategy statements (corporate plans) in the context of Government policy generally and DOE's own statement, *Operational Strategy*.

1.12 In the DOE *Operational Strategy*, the importance of developing co-operation, partnership and better working arrangements with local government at all levels is stressed. The new approach in this Programme, at both council and management levels, will enable much more meaningful arrangements of this kind to be put in place; the Programme sets out specific proposals for this.

1.13 The successful implementation of measures to secure a greater focus by local authorities on policy and strategy will require a willingness to reconsider long established approaches and practices and, where these are no longer appropriate, to embrace with enthusiasm new ideas and new ways of doing things. This Programme sets out the way forward. The SMI process provides the framework in which this can be done but it must be supported by the development of approaches which foster creative thinking and encourage initiative in all aspects of local authority business and at all levels of the organisation.

1.14 In the process of renewal, the value of partnership which has operated successfully at national level with sectoral and other interests must be recognised, as must the need to adapt to changing public expectations of participation. The provision of quality services to the citizen, with emphasis on improving performance, efficiency and value for money is an essential goal of modern public organisations: central, local or semi-state. Action in this regard has already been instigated through the SMI. In line with this policy, a culture of quality service must become central to all public bodies and be seen to be so. Local councillors, managers and staff all face the challenge of managing change and adjusting to a rapidly changing society.

Core principles

1.15   The Programme is based on the following core principles -

- **Enhancing local democracy** by ensuring that
  - local communities and their representatives have a real say in the delivery of the full range of public services locally,
  - new forms of participation by local communities in the decision-making processes of local councils are facilitated,
  - the role of councillors in running local councils is strengthened, and
  - demarcations between town and county authorities are broken down.

- **Serving the customer better** through
  - a focus on the needs of the customer,
  - timely delivery of services of high quality, measured against performance indicators,
  - personnel training and development in customer care,
  - rigorous but streamlined operation of the various regulatory controls, and
  - more openness and transparency in decision-making in local authorities.

- **Developing efficiency** through
  - a modern and progressive financial accounting system with an increased emphasis on costing services,
  - development of performance and financial indicators and value for money audit,
  - development of strategic management,
  - development of partnership between central and local authorities, and between local authorities and other local organisations, and
  - effective use of information technology on a planned basis.

- **Providing proper resources** through
  - the introduction of a source of revenue with in-built buoyancy and a measure of local discretion, and
  - continuing Government support for the restoration of the non-national roads system.

These core principles run through the whole Programme and underpin the measures described in the various chapters.

Conclusion

1.16   In charting the future direction of local government, the Programme seeks to move progressively towards a system which provides efficient services; embraces local development in all its forms; has an input to other public bodies whose actions impact locally; and the strength of which lies in its local democratic mandate and genuine partnership with the local community. The Programme is a long-term one, but it sets out a framework of specific actions to achieve its objectives. Some of these are already under way; others will commence shortly and some will take more time to develop. However, the future direction, the overall approach and the specific actions to be undertaken are set out in this Programme. It sets a clear path to the future for the progressive renewal of local government.

Chapter 2 **Enhancing Democracy**

Introduction

2.1 Local authorities are the only bodies outside of the Dáil whose members are democratically elected by all of the people. This gives local government a status which distinguishes it from all other agencies - public, private or voluntary. In contrast to functionally organised government departments and other public agencies - many of them single purpose agencies - it is locality-based, has a broad range of functions and has a concern and identification with its area. This concern goes beyond the particular services delivered by local government to encompass the general welfare and overall development of the local area and its community.

2.2 Nonetheless, Irish local government is in a relatively weak position when compared with many other European countries where local government provides a wide range of services - education, health, welfare, enterprise development, environmental protection, physical infrastructure, transport, etc. From the experience of these countries, it is clear - even allowing for differences of scale in some cases - that the role of local government can be far greater than it is at present in Ireland. Irish local government has a narrow range of functions, mainly infrastructural, regulatory, environmental, emergency and recreational. Its sole social function is housing.

2.3 To date, local government in Ireland has rarely been accorded a status commensurate with its democratic mandate or been accepted fully as a valid partner in the process of government. Historically, Irish local government developed largely from a judicial system introduced under a colonial regime and from town corporations with limited community involvement. It tends therefore to lack the deep community roots that go to form the basis of continental local government - which evolved over time and predated national governments as widely accepted representative institutions. A primary aim of this Programme is to start a process which will renew our system of local government and its position vis-á-vis central Government and in society generally, so that over time it will come to be more fully accepted as the legitimate voice of local communities, and to be recognised as such within the overall system of government and public administration. Given the present starting point, such objectives are indeed ambitious in the Irish context. If they are to be realised, fundamental change is called for on the part of both central and local government.

2.4 Local authorities are among a number of organisations at work in the development of local areas and communities. At the national level, partnership between Government and the social partners has provided the basis for sound economic and social progress with the support of successive governments and of all political parties. In an increasingly complex world, if local government is to become a key focus and a leader for local communities, it too will need to embrace new concepts of partnership and participation involving voluntary bodies and other local groups. Action along these lines is already evidenced by co-operation with voluntary bodies in the provision of social housing and with the public, private and community sectors in urban and village renewal. The future of local government lies with such partnerships and not in isolation.

2.5   The measures set out in this chapter aim to:

- recognise the legitimacy of local government as a democratic institution;

- enhance the electoral mandate within local government; and

- broaden involvement in local government.

These aims are central to the renewal of the local government system. They are also particularly relevant if local government is to have a meaningful role in local development in partnership with the relevant groups, and to the other steps to broaden its remit (see chapter 3). Taken together, all of these measures are intended to tilt the balance in favour of local government.

2.6   Appendix 1 contains a short outline of the local government system, appendix 2 some statistical data and appendix 3 a list of the local development agencies and community groups receiving support under the *Operational Programme: Local Urban and Rural Development 1994 - 1999* (OPLURD) and under the LEADER II Programme.

Constitutional recognition of local government

2.7   While local government is the subject of a large body of Irish law, it has no constitutional recognition. Almost the only reference to local government in Bunreacht na hÉireann is the right of county and city councils to nominate candidates in a presidential election.

2.8   The recent *Report of the Constitution Review Group* recommended that there should in principle be some form of recognition of local government inserted in the Constitution. The DOE had made a submission to the group supporting such an approach, and the 1991 *Report of the Advisory Expert Committee on Local Government Reorganisation* also made a similar recommendation. Constitutional recognition, as applies in many other countries, would support the role of local government as a democratic institution and a partner in the overall system of government. It would also be very much in keeping with the European Charter of Local Self Government.

2.9   The Government supports the recommendation of the Constitution Review Group. The Minister for the Environment has therefore asked the All-Party Oireachtas Committee on the Constitution, which is considering the report of the group, to consider the inclusion of a provision for constitutional recognition of local government along the lines recommended.

European Charter of Local Self Government

2.10   The European Charter of Local Self Government is an international treaty of the Council of Europe of which Ireland is a founder member. The Charter embodies in broad terms a set of principles to underpin local government in Europe. As such, it has become a benchmark for local government, by setting out general norms to protect and develop its rights and freedoms.

2.11 In recent years, legislation has widened the discretion and generally strengthened the position of local government in Ireland. These measures included the introduction of a power of general competence, the recognition of the representational role of local authority members, a new financial support system for councillors, statutory recognition of local government associations, moves to emphasise the distinctive nature of local authority membership, devolution of various functions and the removal of a wide range of statutory and other controls affecting local authorities. These measures have tended to move our system more into line with the provisions of the Charter. The autonomy of local authorities will be further strengthened by the measures set out in this Programme.

2.12 The Government has therefore decided that Ireland should sign and ratify the Charter as soon as the necessary formalities can be completed. This move represents a clear expression of a genuine commitment to the renewal of local government in our country.

National Economic and Social Council

2.13 The main task of the National Economic and Social Council (NESC) is to provide a forum for discussion of the principles relating to the efficient development of the national economy and the achievement of social justice, and to advise the Government on the application of these principles. The recent work of the Council has covered a wide range of matters and issues directly touching local government, such as local development and institutional arrangements. It is appropriate, therefore, that local government should be in a position to provide a direct input to this work.

2.14 In keeping with the spirit of central/local partnership, the local government sector will therefore be accorded representation on NESC in the near future.

AN ENHANCED ROLE FOR THE COUNCILLOR

2.15 The Government has already decided that there should be an enhancement of the role of councillors in setting policy for local services and in giving leadership to socio-economic development at local level in concert with the social partners. This Programme aims at giving concrete expression to this decision by:

- strengthening the corporate position of councillors within local government, supported by the active involvement of sectoral interests;
- improving administrative support and back-up for carrying out their corporate role; and
- widening the remit of local government.

Present system

2.16 Within the local government system, major decisions of policy (the annual budget, the development plan, the waste management plan, the scheme of letting priorities, etc) rest with councillors who were intended to exercise a pre-eminent role. The implementation or executive role of day-to-day management rests with a chief executive, the county or city manager who is appointed for a seven year term. Functions performed by the councillors are known as reserved functions; a wide range of these are specified across an extensive body of local government law. This framework of reserved/executive functions is also coupled with a range of powers available to councillors to oversee the direction of local authority affairs. Under these general powers they can for example:

- require the manager to inform the council before performing any specified executive function (other than in respect of staff) in a particular instance, or generally;

- require the manager to submit plans, specifications and cost estimates of particular works;

- prohibit the undertaking of new works;

- oversee proposals for land disposal which must be submitted for approval;

- require that a particular act, matter or thing be done by the manager;

- impose restrictions on variations in the numbers of staff or their general rates of remuneration;

- undertake, through an estimates committee, the preparation of the local authority's estimates; and

- ultimately, suspend and remove the manager.

Councillors can also obtain information from the manager on any business or transaction of the authority, can inspect the manager's orders (which set out executive decisions) and can require the manager's attendance at a meeting of the council.

2.17 This reserved/executive framework was originally introduced to bring professionalism and efficiency into the administration of the business of local authorities. A working group of councillors, local authority managers and DOE representatives concluded in 1992 that the general allocation of roles in the reserved/executive framework is essentially correct. A similar system is being introduced for health boards by the Health (Amendment) (No. 3) Act, 1996, is also proposed for the regional education boards in the white paper on education *Charting Our Education Future* and for the re-structured vocational education committees.

Need for change

2.18 While the law envisages councillors exercising the policy-making role, the current dynamics of local government organisation make it difficult for councillors to fulfil that function, other than by the formal adoption of statutory policy documents prepared by management. With the increased emphasis this Programme will bring to bear on quality of service and efficiency, there is a corresponding need for a re-orientation in the corporate role of councillors. They should have a better and more focused involvement in the development of policy generally, and of broad strategy for the major areas of local authority activity. They should also be more involved in the strategic monitoring of local authority operations. A new strategic role of this kind flows naturally from the existing policy role, as expressed in the wide range of specific reserved functions and the range of general powers available to councillors. Essentially, the new strategic role proposed in the following paragraphs should greatly support members in their role as a board of directors and in overseeing local authority affairs.

Strategic policy committees

2.19 In only a very few cases can the current local authority committee structures be seen to represent a coherent framework for the discharge of business. In some instances, large numbers of disparate committees are operating, set up over time to meet the growth in local authority business, to deal with what were then new priorities or with issues which, at that particular point, were of particular significance. These arrangements, which evolved over a long period, and generally in an unplanned way, should now be reformed if the full potential of the role envisaged for councillors is to be realised. The key to developing the policy role of councillors is through a radical overhaul of the existing committee structure on the following lines (see diagram page 21)–

- Each county and city authority and the larger urban authorities will be required to establish strategic policy committees (SPCs) mirroring the major functions of the local authority.

- The number of SPCs will be tailored to the size of the local authority, but should be between two and five; in the smaller authorities, therefore, each SPC would cover several functional areas.

- Each SPC will be supported by the programme manager for the relevant service (see chapter 6), who will operate under the general direction of the committee and submit policy review papers for the service or services in question. This will give a clear focus to the work of the committee and allow it to play a major role in the development of corporate policy and in the local SMI process.

- Within this framework, SPCs can identify particular policy areas for special consideration, arrange for their in-depth examination and report on necessary changes to the full council. The authority's annual report will include material specifically dealing with the work of the SPCs.

- The chairperson of each SPC will be paid an allowance. His/her term of office will be for a period in excess of one year. The system will also be developed so that there will be an equitable spread of these positions among the various groupings on the council.

- The SPCs will meet at least quarterly and submit a written report to the full council; the chairperson will present the report to the council.

2.20 The establishment of SPCs will allow councillors a more meaningful role in policy review and development and will give the chairperson of the SPC a real role in regard to the particular service. For example, an environment committee, in addition to preparatory work in connection with the statutory functions relating to an air, water quality or waste management plan, will also have an opportunity to consider wider policy issues such as programmes to implement *Local Agenda 21*, sustainability principles in planning policy, energy policies in council activities, or green housekeeping. The SPC system will therefore be aimed at more effective involvement of councillors in developing policies for the council's individual services. It will also offer an opportunity for deeper involvement of councillors in the corporate governance of the local authority.

Corporate policy group

2.21 The cathaoirleach of the authority, working with the chairpersons of the SPCs will form a corporate policy group which will have a key role in developing this wider role for councillors. This group will link the work of the different SPCs, act as a sort of cabinet, and provide a forum where policy positions affecting the whole council can be agreed for submission to the full council. The group, which will be serviced by the county/city manager, will also:

- oversee the preparation of strategy statements under the SMI process;

- monitor performance of the authority overall and in specific areas such as customer service; and

- prepare the budget, where an estimates committee is not in existence.

This group will also include the chairperson of the community and enterprise group which each county/city authority will establish in the context of moving towards a more integrated local government and local development system (see chapter 3).

Partnership and participation

2.22 Economic, social and technological change demand a new kind of response from Government, commerce and civil society. Local government, too, can have a major role to play in this context if it can adapt to these broader patterns of change and replicate the kind of success which has been achieved at the national level with the involvement of the social partners. No single actor - public, private or voluntary body - has the knowledge or resources to tackle problems by unilateral action. Representative democracy can be strengthened by the involvement of local people in a meaningful way in devising new approaches to meet community needs. Such involvement and participation can represent a major resource available to councillors in carrying out their functions.

2.23   To assist councillors in their corporate role, to foster a higher degree of community relevance and local participation and to draw on the expertise of the various sectors, not less than one-third of the members of SPCs will be drawn from bodies relevant to the committee's work. For example, a planning/environment committee could include conservation, construction, industrial, farming and other interests. The involvement of non-councillors in this way is not new; it has applied for many decades - and has worked well - in the case of VECs and for some types of local authority committee (eg library, national monuments). Overall, this approach parallels the partnership model which has operated successfully at national level and its extension now to local government is a logical step.

Implementation of SPC system

2.24   A special group representative of councillors, managers and DOE officials is being established to develop these proposals for the revision of the committee structure to implementation stage.

2.25   SPCs will initially be introduced on a non-statutory basis for county/city authorities and for the larger urbans. Comprehensive new local government legislation (see chapter 7) will include statutory backing for the SPCs developed in the light of experience of their practical operation.

2.26   Action on various other fronts outlined in this Programme (eg performance indicators, more modern accounting systems) will be of major assistance in the operations of SPCs. To assist councillors in their overall monitoring role, the requirement for city managers to circulate a monthly statement of the financial position will be extended to local authorities generally.

2.27   The strengthened policy role which the SPC system will confer on councillors will allow more meaningful dialogue to take place between them and central Government. Structured arrangements will be developed under which networks of the chairpersons of SPCs relating to particular services (for example, the chairpersons of housing SPCs) will meet senior officials of DOE on a regular basis to discuss policy development. This process will assist councillors in carrying out their policy role and provide essential feedback in the development of policies at national level.

2.28   As the new system becomes embedded and in the light of experience of its operation, it is proposed to develop still further the role of the councillor in the corporate governance of the local government system.

Strategic Policy Committees (SPCs)

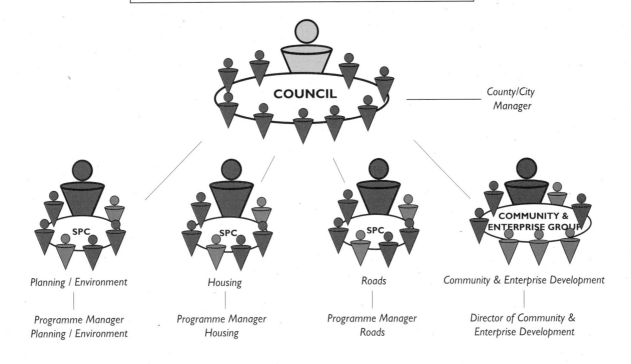

County/City
Manager

Planning / Environment

Programme Manager
Planning / Environment

Housing

Programme Manager
Housing

Roads

Programme Manager
Roads

Community & Enterprise Development

Director of Community &
Enterprise Development

Corporate Policy Group (CPG)

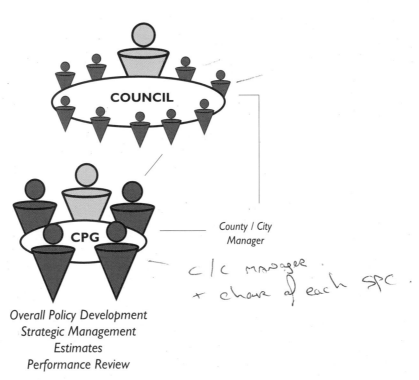

County / City
Manager

c/c manager.
+ chair of each spc.

Overall Policy Development
Strategic Management
Estimates
Performance Review

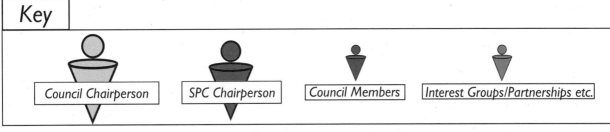

Council Chairperson   SPC Chairperson   Council Members   Interest Groups/Partnerships etc.

Area committees

2.29 The SPC system, and arrangements for broader community involvement set out above, should greatly strengthen the capacity of councillors to fulfil their policy development role. The new system should facilitate the elimination of most other committees relating to specific functions of the local authority. However, elected councillors, in their role as community representatives, have the right and the duty to ensure that policies are translated into the effective delivery of services. Increasingly, local authorities are seeking to decentralise decision-making to the area level through the creation of committees based on the electoral area. This process should be encouraged, though it would not be appropriate to be prescriptive about it, since much will depend on local circumstances. The creation of area committees should enable operational matters to be discussed at that level, leaving the full council free to discuss issues affecting the whole area and policy issues emanating from the SPC system.

Other support measures

2.30 Other measures to support the role of the councillor in the local government system will include:

- the production of a guide to the SMI for councillors by DOE in consultation with the General Council of County Councils (GCCC) later this year, and of a general local government information guide for councillors to be prepared by DOE in 1997;

- the development and strengthening of the arrangements introduced this year for ongoing dialogue and consultation between DOE, the GCCC and the Association of Municipal Authorities of Ireland (AMAI). This process will be extended to other relevant government departments as necessary, each of which will designate a contact person for this purpose. Steps have been taken in recent years to put the members' associations on a more professional footing so as to provide a stronger support role for their member authorities. The GCCC and the AMAI are now statutorily recognised as the representative local government bodies and are in a stronger position to re-orient their own operations and resources towards improved service to the member authorities;

- consideration, in consultation with the representative bodies, of the training and informational needs of councillors generally and of SPC chairpersons in particular. The development of special information/educational modules with the Institute of Public Administration will also be considered in this context; and

- adjustments to the new annual allowance system for councillors to take account of the various measures outlined earlier in this chapter in the course of their implementation. The new system has worked well since its introduction in 1994 and a comprehensive review carried out last year led to a number of improvements.

Local authority representation

2.31 The number of women elected to local authorities is low - about fourteen per cent. This means that a huge potential input to the system is being largely lost. Progress in this area is, however, mainly dependent on action by the political parties in the selection of candidates. The general thrust of this Programme in seeking to make local government more meaningful and relevant to local communities should help to stimulate a wider interest and to attract a correspondingly wider range of prospective candidates and so help to increase the level of women's representation. *address gender imbalance.*

2.32 Since 1991, Ministers and Ministers of State have been disqualified by law from being members of a local authority. For the next local elections this statutory disqualification will apply to other senior office holders at central level (Ceann Comhairle, Cathaoirleach of the Seanad, chairpersons of certain Oireachtas committees) and MEPs. Additionally, Oireachtas members will be disqualified from the positions of cathaoirleach or leas-chathaoirleach of a local authority. Together, these measures are intended to emphasise the distinctive nature of local authority membership. Further actions can be considered in the light of experience following the next local elections.

Conclusion

2.33 The repositioning of the councillor within the local government system will enable him or her to better fulfil the democratic mandate earned through the electoral process. The involvement of sectoral and other interests in the work of local authorities will allow new perspectives and expertise to be brought to bear. The work of councillors will be more challenging and, conversely, councillors will be able to project a more positive image of the work they do. If the work of councillors is seen as more relevant and capable of shaping the policies affecting the everyday lives of their communities, there will undoubtedly be an influx of fresh blood and fresh ideas to local government. And local government will be enriched in the process.

Chapter 3 A Wider Role

The Government believes that a renewed system of local government can provide a more effective focus for the effective delivery of a wider range of public services, for the better development and well being of local communities, and for promoting more local development and enterprise. Partnership and participation can be fostered through local government, and local identity and local loyalties can be harnessed to foster social inclusiveness, equality of opportunity and a tangible sharing of the burdens and rewards of society.

Government Statement - 4 July 1995.

Introduction

3.1　The policy agreement *A Government of Renewal* undertook to renew the system of local government by widening the role of local government generally and, more specifically, by making local authorities the focus for working through local partnerships, county enterprise boards (CEBs), LEADER groups and voluntary and community based bodies. A Devolution Commission was established under the aegis of the Department of the Taoiseach in 1995 and mandated to develop recommendations for a phased programme of devolution and a widening of the role of local government. The Commission's first interim report was published in August 1996.

3.2　There has been significant change in the services delivered by local authorities over the years. A series of measures implemented by successive governments in recent years has extended the functions of local authorities and their range of discretionary powers. However, there have also been counter trends which, at times, have seemed to be at variance with the avowed aims of expanding the role of local government; examples of this are the various local development measures and accompanying new structures.

3.3　The Government has already announced its acceptance of the principles set out by the Devolution Commission that:

- the existing local authority and local development systems should be brought together and simplified;
- people should be provided with the best possible opportunity to participate at local level;
- there is merit in the involvement of the social partners at local level to mirror the success of the partnership concepts at national level;
- there should be maximum co-ordination between agencies at local level to facilitate synergy and to benefit from the experience and work of others so that gaps can be identified and addressed; and
- State agencies should be available for consultation at local level in relation to their actions which have an impact at that level.

3.4   The Government has decided that the local government and local development systems will be integrated on completion of the current round of structural funds programmes. It has also asked the Devolution Commission to report by the end of 1996 on a range of functions suitable for devolution to local government.

Local development initiatives

3.5   Since 1991, there have been several initiatives to stimulate and promote economic and social development at local level, arising initially from the *Programme for Economic and Social Progress* and subsequently as part of EU structural fund programmes.

Partnership companies have been established in urban and rural areas to accelerate local economic and social development and thereby to increase employment and tackle exclusion and marginalisation resulting from long term unemployment, poor educational attainment, poverty and demographic dependency. In all, there are thirty-eight partnership companies; in nine counties the same board implements LEADER and partnership objectives. Typically, a board has eighteen members drawn in equal proportions from the statutory agencies, the social partners and the community sector.

LEADER Groups were set up to promote mainly rural development encompassing the promotion of small and medium-sized enterprises, investment in training, rural tourism and marketing and processing of local produce. There are thirty-six approved LEADER groups with areas varying considerably - part of a county, whole counties and trans-county areas. Board membership varies from five or six to over twenty but it is typically fourteen, with nominees from the community sector, the private sector and State agencies and in some cases supported by a community consultative council.

CEBs

County Enterprise Boards dating from 1993, provide a range of enterprise support services at local level to new and existing businesses, community groups, individual entrepreneurs etc. There are thirty-five boards, all operating within county/city boundaries. Typically, each board has fourteen members drawn from State agencies, social partners, local government and the community sector.

CTCs

County Tourism Committees stimulate and co-ordinate projects in the tourism sector by identifying, influencing and bringing forward new projects and initiatives in their operational areas, and by formulating county tourism action plans for incorporation into county enterprise board action plans and regional tourism organisation plans. There are twenty-five committees, all operating within county/city boundaries. On average, each committee has twenty members drawn from tourism and related sectoral interests, including local government.

CSGs

County Strategy Groups were set up in 1995 to provide co-ordinating mechanisms in each county for the local development initiatives mentioned above; there are thirty such groups. Each group has eight members on average, comprising the chairpersons of partnership companies, the CEB, LEADER groups, the county tourism committee and representatives of local government.

3.6   These initiatives have reflected the spirit of partnership which has underpinned economic and social development at national level for the past nine years. A key to their success is that they have been highly innovative in their working methods and in preparing flexible, targeted and integrated responses to local needs. Much of local development is structural funds led and the reality is that the various categories of structural funding have required separate and discrete funding and reporting arrangements.

3.7   The local development organisations share a common approach in achieving their objectives. The key elements of this approach are:

- an area-based approach to tackling local problems tailored to the particular needs and resources of the area;

- a multi-sectoral approach to addressing problems, which involves participants from the public, private and voluntary sectors;

- new patterns of involvement by national and local public authorities, supported by flexible and innovative staffing arrangements;

- a strategic approach to developing local potential, with a strong emphasis on integrated planning and implementation;

- providing local structures with the necessary resources and authority to achieve their strategic objectives;

- co-ordination of national policies to ensure coherence of policy-making and commitment to policy change and subsidiarity; and

- effective linkages between local and central structures to ensure that difficulties identified at local level shape central policy making.

Local government and local development

3.8   The local development initiatives, as originally launched, did not relate significantly to local government which, given its existing administrative structures and comprehensive geographical spread, in different circumstances might have been considered the appropriate base. The limited financial resources available to local authorities, the demands of the traditional services and the lack of buoyancy in their financing system were seen to limit their capacity to take a wider role in community development. The improved funding arrangements for local government now being put in place (see chapter 5) should allow more scope for an increased local authority role.

3.9   As already indicated, the local development initiatives have developed flexible, targeted and integrated responses to local needs, and have achieved considerable success in their individual fields of endeavour. However, there is criticism of the numbers as well as the complexity of the structures which have been established; there can sometimes seem to be a confusing multiplicity of organisations, with overlapping functions, giving rise to duplication of services and of administration, and some confusion for potential clients. These concerns were reflected in a recent review of the Irish local development experience by the OECD. However, the OECD also emphasised the exciting potential of the Irish partnership approach to local development, especially through the wide base of participants and their integrated approach. They found that the empowerment of local communities involved has enabled them to take responsibility for their own affairs in an important exercise in participative democracy. There is a strong case, therefore, for greater integration, simplification and reorganisation in a way which retains and strengthens the essence of the local development experience. Accordingly, the Government has decided that, on completion of the current round of spending under the EU Community Support Framework for Ireland (ie from 1 January 2000), an integrated local government and local development system will come into place.

3.10   Planning will now commence towards that new system so that, by a series of progressive measures up to the year 2000, each system will progressively move closer towards, and assist and support, the other, while recognising the strengths of each and exploiting the opportunities presented for synergy and joint action.

To assist the process of integration, therefore, the following measures will be implemented to facilitate the planning of the new system and to develop more structured relations between both systems in the interim -

- Each county/city authority will appoint a director of community and enterprise development.

- Each county/city authority will establish a Community and Enterprise Group (CEG) with not less than half the members drawn from the local development bodies and equality of status for all members. The CEGs will replace and carry on the co-ordinating role of the county strategy groups established under OPLURD and will be charged with promoting co-ordination generally between the two systems and steps towards their integration. Specific tasks will, where necessary, be assigned to sub-committees of the CEG.

- There will be increased collaboration and joint working in relation to specific projects and operational issues, where the opportunity for this exists. Joint working groups are already being established in relation to housing estate management and there has also been successful collaborative action on urban and village renewal. Further specific areas for meaningful co-operation will be identified by CEGs.

- Familiarisation/information programmes will be put in place for local government staff and councillors in relation to local development initiatives, and for the staff and board members of local development organisations in relation to local government. Local authorities, in particular, will need to adapt to new methods of organisation and a broad range of non traditional methods in dealing with local development coalitions concerned with issues such as social exclusion.

3.11   Continued support for local development at central level will be maintained and co-ordinated by the Minister of State for European Affairs and Local Development.

Framework for integration

3.12   It is important, in bringing local government and the local development bodies together by the year 2000, that an over-prescriptive approach is avoided and that arrangements best suited to each area should be allowed to emerge. Each CEG will, therefore, be charged with the task of developing, before the end of 1997, a fully worked out plan of how best to achieve integration of the two systems in its area. Integration will have to respect the following principles -

- Duplication of roles and administrative systems must be eliminated.

- The partnership approach involving the community, social partners and State agencies on a multi-sectoral basis must remain part of the system.

- There must be continued attention to problems of social exclusion, with intensive programmes across a range of services.

- Comprehensive community and enterprise development plans, including the continuation of local area action plans, must be an integral part of the new system, with the full co-operation of all the social partners.

- The one stop shop concept should be developed to the maximum extent possible, especially by pursuing the development of community based resources.

Further steps to extend the remit of local government

3.13 Pending recommendations by the Devolution Commission on a range of functions suitable for devolution to local authorities, the following measures will be taken to further extend the remit of local government -

- Recognising the legitimacy of the local authorities' role in representing and articulating the needs and concerns of their areas, State agencies will be available for consultation at local level in relation to their actions which have an impact at that level. Appropriate personnel will be available (to attend local authority meetings where necessary) to discuss issues arising in relation to the policies and programmes of their agencies. The Department of the Taoiseach will shortly be advising public agencies of Government policy in this regard.

- Arrangements have already been made for the establishment of working groups of local authority housing officials and representatives from local partnership companies to tackle issues of housing estate management and development. This type of approach is particularly appropriate for issues which are of joint concern to a number of agencies, for example in the area of community development or drug abuse. Public bodies and local authorities will be encouraged to establish other multi-agency working groups of this kind under the aegis of the local authority to deal with other issues of joint concern. These groups will co-ordinate working arrangements and maximise organisational effort and resources.

- It is proposed to establish special committees to facilitate liaison between local authorities and the Gardaí on a structured basis. These committees will provide a mechanism for an exchange of views on issues of common concern (but obviously excluding specific security and investigative issues). They will be in a position, therefore, to consider a wide range of matters including traffic, vandalism, planning for events attracting large crowds, community-based crime prevention programmes, and other matters affecting peace and good order within the community. The aim is that these liaison procedures will commence early in 1997 and planning for this has already begun.

- Representation of local councillors on the boards of relevant public agencies whose operations affect local areas will be continued. In keeping with this policy, local councillors will be included on the proposed regional education boards and on the boards of directors of the new harbour companies.

Conclusion

3.14   A renewed system of local government will provide a more effective focus for the better delivery of a range of public services. The measures proposed to integrate the local government and local development systems will strengthen the local government system and, at the same time, build on the lessons learned from the local development innovations. The establishment of more structured mechanisms for interaction between local authorities and other State agencies will lead to more informed decision-making on the part of State agencies and of local authorities and will accelerate the development of unified approaches to issues of joint concern, thereby maximising organisational effort and resources in addressing local needs and priorities.

Chapter 4 **Quality Services**

The aim will be to achieve and demonstrate value for money, high standards of service, efficiency, courtesy and accountability. A central objective will be to assert the authority of the consumer/client of public services.

A Government of Renewal

Introduction

4.1 The Government is committed to renewing public confidence in the system of government by the introduction of reforms in the delivery of public services. The type of public service which the Government is working to achieve can be summed up in one word: quality. Ireland needs and deserves a public service which operates to the highest standards, both in the quality of its decision-making and in the quality of service provided at the point of impact on the customer. This quality imperative applies to all levels of government.

4.2 If local government is to assume a wider role at the local level as envisaged in this Programme and as an important element in the democratic process, it is essential that it delivers a quality service in all its operations. The public will quite rightly judge the suitability of local authorities for additional functions and responsibilities by the performance of councillors, management and staff.

4.3 Government, including local government, exists to serve the people. However, in the public service there is a danger that insufficient attention may be paid to the needs of the customer and that the internal demands, preferences and perceptions of the organisation may take precedence. To counteract this, there is a need to establish systems to ensure that those responsible for the delivery of services are driven by the requirements of customer needs and customer satisfaction and that services are viewed from the customer's, rather than the organisation's, perspective. In this way, government is made more responsive and the customer is better served.

4.4 Local authorities do not always receive adequate recognition for the good work that they do. In fact, it may be that, given the nature of the services that local authorities provide (water supply, refuse collection, development control, etc), people will generally only pay attention to the quality of local authority services when a matter arises which affects them directly at an individual level or when there is a breakdown in service.

4.5 While there have been many worthwhile measures to improve the quality of services provided by local authorities in recent years, action is now required to widen and deepen the concern to meet the needs of the customer. This Programme, therefore, seeks to promote the development of fully customer-oriented services in local authorities, building on the many good aspects of local authority services while at the same time setting out an agenda for change.

4.6   The following are areas for action on quality -

- Ethos and culture: ensuring that there is a commitment throughout the organisation to customer-service quality values.

- Co-ordination: cutting across administrative divisions or departments and working with other organisations to promote more co-ordinated delivery of services to customers.

- Decentralisation: breaking down large, centralised services into smaller, more accessible units, closer and more responsive to customers.

- Reception: improving the conditions of direct customer/provider contact.

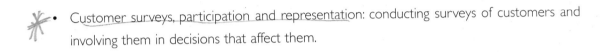
- Customer surveys, participation and representation: conducting surveys of customers and involving them in decisions that affect them.

- Complaints procedures: setting up mechanisms to provide for customer redress.

- Setting standards: developing quantifiable performance indicators and related standards.

- Information: improving the availability and nature of information for customers about public services. Fo'

- Simplification: reducing complexities related to rules, procedures and official forms.

- Human resources management: introducing training and incentive schemes specifically to promote customer responsive services; encouraging two-way communication by setting up mechanisms to enable staff to communicate more effectively with management; and giving staff in closest contact with the customer greater autonomy in decision-making as well as greater responsibility.

The following paragraphs set out ideas for specific action by local authorities to enhance the quality of service as well as details of action necessary at central Government level to encourage and assist this process.

Ethos and culture

4.7   The aim must be to develop an ethos and a culture in the public sector, including local authorities, which gives primacy to the needs of the customer and supports a continuous search for ways to enhance the quality of service.

Experience suggests that certain key principles must be adhered to if this ethos and culture is to develop and lasting quality improvements are to be secured:

- Staff should be involved at all stages in developing and implementing quality improvements and there should be appropriate consultations with staff interests.

- The leaders of the organisation must be committed to the achievement of quality services.

4.8 The SMI process now being undertaken by local authorities, together with implementation of the agenda for quality outlined in this Programme, will contribute significantly to the development of a more customer-driven ethos and culture in local government. But it is primarily a matter for local authorities themselves to develop and implement plans for quality improvements in accordance with their own local circumstances and priorities.

One stop shop centres

4.9 The efficient provision of a high quality service to the public requires integrated, customer-oriented services. However, the customer does not necessarily differentiate between the various public sector organisations and may not always appreciate 'who does what'. The question of linkage between local authorities and other public services must, therefore, be addressed. Ideally, there should be a single local contact point where people can get information and advice on the full range of public services, submit claims or applications for such services, and receive the services required. The idea of one stop shop centres for consumers of local authority services, town and county, is addressed in chapter 7.

4.10 Some public services (eg the Revenue Commissioners, the Department of Social Welfare) have made significant progress towards developing one stop shops covering their own particular services. Various other related initiatives are under way, including pilot projects in the context of western development, work on the establishment of an integrated social services system, and on the development of local authority centres with comprehensive information and advice on housing options and schemes. As yet, however, limited progress has been made towards development of the type of 'gateway to government' envisaged above. Local authorities, with their multi-purpose remit and wide geographical coverage, are well placed to fulfil this role, building on the existing network of local authority area offices.

4.11 Every opportunity should be taken to locate public offices either in the same building - a one stop shop centre - or in close proximity to one another - a public service cluster. Local authority proposals relating to office accommodation will in future be assessed on this basis. All other public agencies are being encouraged by Government to take full account of this objective in determining how to meet their accommodation needs. This policy is necessarily a long-term one but every opportunity which arises should be availed of to move progressively in this direction, both to the maximum extent within local government, and on the broader front. While the ultimate objective is to cover the full range of public services, it is particularly desirable that local authority officials dealing with development issues and other local development agencies (county enterprise boards, LEADER groups, partnership companies, FÁS) should be located close to one another. The same principle applies to the other functions of the local authorities - for example, the housing section of the local authority should be located close to health board and social welfare offices.

4.12 The progress which can be made in relation to one stop shop centres will vary according to local circumstances and needs. Where new accommodation is required for services provided directly to the public, or where existing accommodation is being substantially upgraded, it will be relatively easy to change to a one stop shop centre. In other cases, the more limited, yet worthwhile, steps of assigning officials from other agencies to work in local authority offices, or the provision of information about other public services in local authority offices, should be considered for the short term. Actions in this area will need to be co-ordinated with developments by other public agencies such as the Department of Social Welfare.

4.13 A number of local authorities have already shown interest in taking initiatives in the development of one stop shop centres which will have linkages with other locally-based public services. Pilot projects will be availed of to determine the best approaches. High level local project teams will be established, under the aegis of the local authorities concerned and comprising representatives of other local public services, to develop suitable proposals within six months and to oversee their implementation. The project teams will take full account of, and build on, existing initiatives in this area.

Decentralisation

4.14 Decentralisation of service delivery is at present being considered by a number of local authorities. This will generally involve: the physical relocation of services from headquarters within a city or county to a number of local offices; the use of more flexible forms of management and work organisation (teamwork) in those offices; devolution of service delivery functions to those offices; and the consequent freeing-up of headquarters to concentrate on broader policy issues. This general approach is already being pursued by Donegal County Council. Implementation of decentralisation measures will need to take account of the proposed one stop shop centres so that they are used, where appropriate, as the basis for decentralised service delivery. DOE will monitor progress with these initiatives, assisting where possible to secure successful implementation.

Public offices

4.15 The design, appearance and functioning of local authority public offices should be to the highest standard. In practical terms, this means, for example, that hatches should no longer be used, that the facilities should allow the right to privacy to be respected, that offices should be well-maintained, that modern queuing arrangements should be used and that buildings should be accessible to people with disabilities. Many local authorities have made significant improvements in the standards of their public offices in recent years but there are some areas where there is still considerable scope for improvement. The new funding arrangements for local authorities outlined in this Programme should help to widen the scope for action.

Co-ordination of service delivery

4.16   Traditionally, local authorities have delivered services on a functional basis; the roads department looking after roads, the housing department looking after housing, the parks department looking after parks and open spaces, and so on. Co-ordination between departments in the delivery of services to individual areas has tended to be weak, particularly in the larger local government areas. However, in recent years many local authorities have been improving co-ordination through mechanisms such as the development of local offices, the establishment of a local authority presence in individual areas (estate officers), more frequent area visits by administrative and technical staff, greater sharing of information between relevant departments and greater emphasis on teamwork and co-ordination meetings. The benefits of increased co-ordination have been recognised and there is scope for continuing evolution and development of co-ordinating mechanisms in local authorities generally.

Customer consultation and complaints procedures

4.17   More structured and systematic approaches to consulting customers would have obvious benefits for local authorities. There is a variety of techniques available, including customer panels/advisory groups, market research and comment cards. Such techniques allow local authorities to find out what customers really think about matters such as opening hours in public offices, the speed of service, the standard of office accommodation, the level of courtesy shown and the overall level of service. They also enable customers to suggest improvements. Already, market research has been availed of by some local authorities, for example by Dun Laoghaire-Rathdown and Westmeath County Councils.

4.18   If people have dealings with their local authority only infrequently, it is all the more important that they receive a quality service when they are in contact. This applies, in particular, if the purpose of the contact is to express dissatisfaction about some aspect of a service. How an organisation responds to a complaint can make a lasting impact on how it is perceived. The establishment of clear and unambiguous procedures for dealing quickly and effectively with complaints can make a major contribution to improving the quality of service; such procedures might include assigning responsibility for dealing with complaints to particular staff members, establishing arrangements for monitoring progress, and setting time limits within which responses should be finalised.

Performance indicators and service standards

4.19   A common feature of measures to improve quality of service is the setting, and meeting, of customer service standards. These involve the use of performance indicators (the yardstick by which quality is to be judged), standards themselves (the quality level to be achieved) and measurement of actual performance (achievement compared to standards). Performance indicators and the related standards need to be relevant to key areas of customer concern, need to be clear and well-defined, and responsive to changes in the quality of service.

4.20 As part of the SMI process, a wide range of performance indicators has been suggested to local authorities by DOE for use in the development of strategy statements and the associated action plans. Some indicators are already used by local authorities in their management of particular services (in roads and housing for example) and by DOE in its role in relation to individual programmes.

4.21 To foster greater emphasis on achieving real improvement in performance, local authorities will be asked to set standards in respect of a number of performance indicators and to measure progress in relation to those standards. A special working group will be set up comprising representatives of local authorities and DOE, including the VFM unit, to identify a number of key areas of local authority performance and suggest standards for those areas. Such areas could include for example:

- the proportion of planning applications determined within two months of receipt and the proportion deferred;

- length of time taken to issue motor tax discs and driver licences;

- length of time to let vacant local authority houses; and

- response to requests for environmental information.

Local authorities will be required to publish details of their performance against the standards. This will greatly enhance transparency in the local government system and, when taken with the preparation and publication of financial performance indicators as proposed in chapter 5, will be a powerful stimulus to efficiency in the system.

Information

4.22 A large amount of information is already provided to the public on local authority business. For example:

- the physical planning system includes provision for giving public notice of planning applications, public inspection of planning registers and documentation, giving reasons for decisions, and notification of rights of appeal;

- local authorities maintain registers of air and water pollution licences to which the public have access; and

• • city and county authorities are required since 1991 to prepare, and make publicly available, annual reports on their operations during the year.

In addition, DOE publishes a large amount of information of relevance to the local government system, including sets of leaflets suitable for use and distribution at local authority offices.

4.23   There are, nevertheless, issues to be addressed. In particular, while the Access to Information on the Environment Regulations give the public important new rights of access to environmental information held by public authorities, the Ombudsman has expressed concern on a number of occasions about the responses of individual local authorities to the obligations placed on them. Problems relate both to reluctance to make certain information available and the length of time taken to comply with requests. There is scope, therefore, to embrace more fully the concept of openness and transparency in the conduct of business.

4.24   The law on local authority meetings is being modernised and consolidated, with the aim of making comprehensive new regulations in the near future. These will include a statutory right for members of the public to attend council meetings.

4.25   To let people know what they are entitled to by way of information from local authorities, DOE will prepare and publish a comprehensive list of public rights to information. These rights will be enhanced further by the proposed Freedom of Information legislation which will apply to local authorities.

4.26   There is scope to improve the level and quality of information provided about local authority operations. For example, the general public are often unaware of the full range of services provided by local authorities, how services can be availed of, and their obligations and duties as customers. More can be done to inform people in situations where services have to be interrupted and there is likely to be significant temporary inconvenience. Similarly, local authorities could do more to highlight the good work that they do and their positive achievements in the service of the local community. Too often, information is presented in unnecessarily complicated, archaic or legalistic language and does not take proper account of the perspective of the recipient.

4.27   Measures which can be taken to address these issues include the preparation of guides detailing the range of local authority services and how they may be accessed - such guides have already been produced by some authorities. Greater use might also be made of media such as information leaflets, periodic newsletters, local radio, and the Internet. Local authorities should consider the development of a more pro-active approach to the giving of information and greater targeting of information at those to whom it is relevant. The involvement of users in the preparation of forms, leaflets, and notices will lead to greater clarity and understanding.

4.28   The content and presentation of local authority annual reports will be reviewed by DOE, in consultation with local authorities, to see what improvements might be made. The review will focus on questions such as how to make reports more relevant to the customer.

Seirbhísí as Gaeilge

4.29   Is cuid riachtanach de sheirbhís den scoth an teacht atá ar sheirbhísí as Gaeilge. Tá na h-údaráis áitiúla ar thús cadhnaíochta i measc na n-údarás poiblí ó thaobh bearta a chur chun tosaigh a chuireann ar chumas daoine ar mian leo a gcuid gnóthaí a dhéanamh trí mheán na Gaeilge a leithéid a dhéanamh. Tá bunáite na n-údarás áitiúil tar éis Oifigeach Gaeilge a cheapadh le plean cuimsitheach gníomhaíochta a réiteach ina leith seo. Tá saothar na n-údarás áitiúil sa réimse seo á chomhordú ag an nGrúpa Stiúrtha, a bhunaigh an Roinn Comhshaoil. Níos túisce i mbliana, d'fhoilsigh an Grúpa moltaí leasaithe chun úsáid na Gaeilge a chur chun cinn agus le seirbhísí dátheangacha a fhorbairt. Leanfaidh an Grúpa Stiúrtha de bheith ag cothú ghníomhaíocht na n-údarás áitiúil ar an gcaoi seo.

Review of the operation of regulatory controls

4.30   Regulatory controls for which local authorities are responsible include the development control system, building regulations and fire safety provisions. These and other such controls serve important objectives of public policy and must be rigorously enforced by local authorities. There is, nevertheless, scope to review the manner of their implementation at local level so as to ensure that essential requirements are always fully and clearly set out, that compliance is made as simple and straightforward as possible, that the requirements decided upon are fully justified in the circumstances of each case, and that decisions are given in a reasonable and definite timeframe.

Information technology

4.31   Information technology (IT) can play a major role in supporting the development of services closer to the customer and improving the quality of service. For instance, IT can:

- provide staff in devolved offices and one stop shop centres with relevant, easily accessible data which they can use to serve the customer;

- improve direct access by the public to information, in local authority offices or elsewhere, on a wide range of topics including planning applications, council meeting agendas, environmental matters;

- disseminate information to a wide audience (via the development of more local government sites on the Internet); and

- allow the creation of systems to track complaints and monitor responses to them.

4.32   There are other important ways in which IT can be used to improve quality of service. IT is essential to ensure that adequate management information is available for decisions on resource allocation, the management of individual projects and budgeting/accounting. In addition, the use of modern IT facilities means that administrative tasks can be carried out differently and more effectively. Workgroup computing (using software products now available) also facilitates the introduction of flatter organisational structures, encouraging the teamwork approach which is conducive to quality service.

Human resources management

4.33   The issue of quality in local authority services cannot be viewed in isolation from other aspects of local government renewal. In particular, the achievement of significant and sustained quality improvements will be closely related to changes in human resources management practice. Issues such as training and delegation are addressed in chapter 6.

Quality initiatives

4.34   The Convention on Quality in Local Government, which was held in Dublin Castle in June 1996 was organised by DOE and attended by some 300 representatives of local authorities. It highlighted the need for a quality approach to local government services through presentations by representatives of organisations which have dealings with local authorities on a regular basis, by leaders of organisations which have themselves developed major quality initiatives and by individual councillors and managers. The Convention generated positive and constructive ideas for quality initiatives. The papers submitted to the Convention will be published by DOE and made available to local authorities shortly.

4.35   In the framework of SMI, local authorities have been requested to develop specific quality initiatives aimed at improving the quality of services which they provide. In this context, local authorities might explore the possibility of working towards obtaining certification of particular services under formal quality standards; Wexford County Council has already received accreditation under the ISO 9000 series of standards for the quality of the service provided by its motor tax office.

4.36   It is a matter for local authorities to develop their own quality initiatives in accordance with local circumstances and priorities and to set out their intentions in this regard in their SMI strategy statements - different approaches can be adopted to similar issues. Details of initiatives will be published by DOE in a quality bulletin in order to promote best practice among local authorities. In this way, local authorities will learn from each others' experiences and the benefits of the diversity of local government will be maximised.

Quality awards

4.37   While much work has been done by local authorities to improve quality of service, experience shows that achieving significant and sustained quality improvements in any organisation requires special commitment and effort. In recognition of this, an annual quality service awards scheme for local authorities will be inaugurated. Local authorities in 1997 will be invited to submit details of specific quality initiatives which they have undertaken and these will be judged by an independent assessment panel to whom formal presentations will be made by the local authorities involved. Financial awards will be made in 1998 for successful initiatives on the basis of criteria such as:

- an assessment of the previous quality of the service;

- the extent of staff participation in the development and implementation of the proposal;

- the extent of consultation with customers;

- the use of performance indicators and related standards to measure improvements in the quality of the service;

- co-operative arrangements whereby joint action by local authorities, particularly in areas where boundaries intersect, result in improved efficiencies and service to the customer; and

- specific measures/innovations which result in cost reductions/efficiencies.

Local authorities will be expected to utilise the awards to develop and implement further quality initiatives.

Conclusion

4.38 Quality is a key area within this Programme. The enhanced emphasis in local authorities on quality of service will play a major role in improving the general perception of local government and will demonstrate its suitability for the wider role detailed in chapter 3; internally, greater customer satisfaction should lead to increased job satisfaction for local authority employees; and specific quality initiatives can show the way forward. Moreover, quality is an area where the primary onus for action necessarily rests with local authorities themselves. Quality is a means by which local authorities can demonstrate their own commitment to renewal and change.

Chapter 5 **Finance**

The Government will immediately commission a professional study to see how a fair, equitable and reasonable system of funding can be introduced with a view to publishing a White Paper on the subject.

A Government of Renewal

Introduction

5.1 The availability, control and use of finance are at the core of any organisation's existence, not least for local authorities in their public service delivery role. There are growing demands on local authority funding, as the requirement for new and improved services increases, but there is little prospect of meeting these demands from existing resources. Significant current account deficits already exist, estimated to be in the region of IR£120 million overall; while the inclusion of accruals would mean that local authorities are generally solvent, the scale of these deficits is, nevertheless, a matter of concern. At local level, the servicing of overdrafts and other loans arising from deficits reduces the availability of funds to improve services to the customer.

5.2 Lack of buoyancy in income and a narrow funding base mean that, even with a growing economy, there are funding difficulties for local government. As a result, not only are local authorities without funds to respond to worthwhile community projects, they are finding it increasingly difficult simply to maintain present services at acceptable levels. There are particular problems arising in meeting the costs of maintaining new water and waste water treatment plants and of waste disposal.

5.3 A locally available, independent and buoyant source of finance is vital in the renewal process for local authorities to enable them to flourish and meet their customers' essential requirements. The identification of potential sources of local finance and the requirements for the future were the main tasks set for the professional study carried out by KPMG Management Consulting; their report *The Financing of Local Government in Ireland* was published last June. This confirmed that, while a number of options exist for the future funding of local government, none of them is ideal and all of them pose difficulties. Standing still is, however, a poor option. New sources of funding are urgently required by the local authority system, but there is general political and community agreement that the provision of new funding should not involve an increase in the overall burden of taxation.

5.4 The Government has already demonstrated its commitment to improving the resources available to local authorities by providing significant additional monies for the ten year non-national roads restoration programme. In excess of IR£143 million is being provided in State grants for non-national roads in 1996, an increase of IR£36 million on the 1994 level; of this total, IR£73 million is being provided for the restoration programme.

Charges for services

5.5   There are serious difficulties in the manner in which local authorities charge consumers for services provided on an individual basis. A cardinal principle in charging for a service is that the level of charge should vary with usage. This is the system which applies with other services such as electricity, gas supply and telephone. It is also the system which local authorities apply, for the most part, to commercial users of water. Many local authorities also apply the usage principle to charges for domestic refuse collection through bag-tagging or other usage-based schemes. Charges for domestic water supply (and sewerage facilities), however, are either flat charges or are related to broad rateable valuation bands, but never to usage. The KPMG study concluded that metering domestic supplies would be an uneconomic proposition having regard to the revenue generated. The charge for domestic water and sewerage facilities is thus more in the nature of a tax and should, in the Government's view, be consolidated into general taxation. These charges will not therefore be levied in respect of 1997 or following years; charges due for 1996 and earlier years will continue to be payable. The abolition of these charges will also result in cost savings to the local authorities as the administrative, legal and other costs involved will no longer apply.

5.6   The KPMG report identified waste management as an area which will be subject to substantially increased costs for local authorities in the coming years. It is particularly important that waste management policies are directed towards minimising the quantity of waste disposed through landfill. Attainment of national targets for diverting waste from landfill and for recycling can be greatly facilitated through the use of economic and fiscal instruments. Unlike charges for domestic water supply and sewerage facilities, charges for domestic refuse collection can be related to usage, and will be an important instrument in waste management policy. Furthermore, given the complexities of the different arrangements in place, with a mix of privately-run and local authority services, the option must be retained to allow local authorities to continue to provide environmentally safe refuse collection services, while being in a position to defray the costs through charges. To do otherwise could drive more local authorities to privatise the service for purely financial reasons, rather than ensuring that the best decision is reached, taking all factors into account. These charges will therefore remain.

5.7   The revenues foregone by local authorities through the abolition of domestic water and sewerage facilities charges will be replaced in full under the new funding arrangements outlined below which involve the introduction of a new source of funding dedicated entirely to them.

New funding arrangements

5.8   Having considered the options presented in the KPMG report, the Government has decided to opt for a new local revenue system to replace the present Rate Support Grant (RSG) and the revenues generated from domestic water and sewerage facilities charges. From 1 January 1997, the full proceeds of motor taxation (ie the excise duties charged on vehicle licences) will become a dedicated local government revenue source, fully assigned to local authorities. This should provide a buoyant source of income for local authorities into the future as car ownership grows. The basic rates of tax will continue to be set nationally. The new source of funding will come into effect on 1 January 1997 with interim arrangements applying in 1997 to ensure a smooth transition period. However, as it is important that local authorities should have a measure of discretion over the rates of tax, a further change is proposed, with a start date of 1 January 1998 envisaged. Local authorities will be empowered to vary the national rates of tax as they apply to vehicles (other than commercial goods vehicles) by a margin of up to six per cent, subject to a maximum of three per cent in the first year (1998). There will be no increase in motor tax in the interim. Preparatory work on the necessary legislation is commencing immediately. The net effect of these changes is that for 1998, local authorities will be empowered to vary the national rate by up to three per cent and for 1999 and subsequent years by up to a maximum of six per cent.

5.9   These arrangements will need to be tailored to the individual circumstances of each local authority, as:

- motor tax authorities operate at county or city level. There will have to be provision for an equitable sharing of the benefits of the new funding system among all the local authorities;

- the amounts collected by the different motor tax authorities will vary, in some cases significantly, from the income levels generated by the existing system - some will collect considerably more and others considerably less. This will require a transfer of resources to prevent some authorities being adversely affected by the changes; and

- furthermore, in line with the findings of the KPMG report, an equalisation system must be put in place to support the less well-off authorities so that they can provide services at levels comparable with the financially stronger authorities.

5.10   These needs will be met through the following arrangements -

- The motor tax authorities will be required to share out the tax they retain on an equitable basis among the local authorities within their motor tax area (the urban authorities) or with the neighbouring county/city authorities where one authority acts on another's behalf for motor tax collection purposes (as in the case of Cork, Dublin and Galway).

- There will be an equalisation fund into which motor tax authorities will pay the full proceeds of motor tax on commercial goods vehicles and twenty per cent of motor tax on all other vehicles.

- Payments from the equalisation fund will ensure that there will be full restoration of the income foregone by local authorities through the abolition of charges for domestic water and sewerage facilities and the RSG.

These arrangements will operate so that all local authorities, including the urban authorities, will share equitably in the considerable buoyancy that the new funding system will deliver. Work will immediately be initiated to develop during 1997 a more finely-tuned equalisation system for 1998 and subsequent years. This will ensure that the needs and resources of the different local authorities are taken fully into account in the distribution of funds. Interim steps will be taken towards the new system for 1997, on the basis of preliminary analysis to be undertaken over the coming weeks.

5.11 The financial effect of these new arrangements, based on 1996 estimated figures, is set out in the following table:

Domestic Water & Sewerage Facilities Charges	Rate Support Grant	Total	Motor Tax Proceeds (net of collection costs)
IR£53m	IR£193m	IR£246m	IR£258m

Buoyancy in future years, together with the potential income from the local variation element from 1998 onwards and the Government's continued commitment to the non-national roads restoration programme should ensure a margin of comfort for local authorities in the future.

5.12 Given that the new arrangements outlined above will make significant new funds available within the local government sector, it will be important for local authorities to set targets for significant reductions in their deficit levels, with a view to their gradual elimination. Arrangements will be made for consultation and agreements to be reached between DOE and individual local authorities on this issue over the coming months.

Community development contribution

5.13 The report *Towards Cohesive Local Government - Town and County* outlined an innovative approach whereby local authorities could sponsor, either on their own initiative or in partnership with local community or other groups, discretionary developmental projects or programmes which could not otherwise proceed within available financial resources. This would involve a specific project or programme approved by the council where it would be open to the local authority to introduce a community development contribution for a defined period to meet the specific costs involved. This would also help to underpin the partnership approach in assisting local community and other groups. Community projects of the type described above could encompass a whole county/city, or have a more local focus. This would involve co-operative effort by the town council and the area committee of the county council. The community contribution would have to be sufficiently flexible so as to be applied to defined areas within local authorities, or to combined areas involving one or more local authorities. Proposals along these lines will be developed for inclusion in the comprehensive local government legislation referred to in chapter 7.

Capital projects

5.14 Capital programmes have, in the past, operated on the basis of tight central control. Some changes have already been initiated to relax these controls giving local authorities more freedom to decide on priorities and plan activities accordingly.

5.15 In the housing area local authorities have been afforded greater flexibility since the early 1990s to plan and develop social housing projects which satisfy certain unit cost limits without the need for prior approval from DOE.

5.16 As part of the non-national roads restoration programme, each county council has prepared a multi-annual road works programme for the years 1996 - 2000. Implementation of these programmes introduces greater flexibility in the planning, management and execution of road works. Responsibility for identifying and prioritising projects in each programme rests with local authorities.

5.17 In the water services programme, DOE will aim at a more devolved approach to the funding of projects, with local authorities being allocated block grants on a rolling three-year basis. This will give them greater discretion in setting priorities. The devolved approach has already proven successful in the existing small schemes sub-programme. Major water and waste water projects being co-funded under the EU cohesion or structural funds will continue to be dealt with on an individual basis.

5.18 The potential for the relaxation of authorisations, technical and other controls in the smaller centrally funded capital programmes (eg library, fire, swimming pools) is being examined with a view to also streamlining these schemes.

Efficient use of resources

5.19 The measures outlined above will guarantee local authorities a predictable and buoyant source of revenue. This will enable them to reduce deficits, to keep their mainline services at satisfactory levels and to make real improvements in their communities. In return for this, the Government is demanding that local authorities should be seen to optimise their use of resources on a sound businesslike basis.

5.20 Local government spends almost IR£2 billion a year and provides a range of infrastructure critical to Ireland's economic performance. The taxpayer, whether at European, national or local level, needs to be assured that this money is being spent effectively and efficiently. It is, of course, accepted that the nature of some local authority activities precludes a totally commercial approach. For example, houses are let at subsidised rents. But even with those services, local authorities must develop a culture of producing quality outputs at competitive cost levels.

5.21 Local authorities have made considerable efforts to improve efficiencies. The vast bulk of capital spending is carried out by private contractors, on the basis of competitive tendering. The restriction in the funding base of local authorities since the late 1970s has enforced efficiencies. Changes in the accounting system in the 1970s to a programmatic basis reflecting their main functions, moved the system closer to costing principles. What is now required is to set a framework within which the efficiency and value for money agenda will routinely permeate all aspects of financial management.

Financial management system

5.22 The first priority in establishing the efficiency approach is to have financial systems which inform management and the public as to how the local authority is performing. In common with other public service agencies, the original basis of financial management in local authorities was one of accounting for expenditure, supported by rigorous audit procedures. The Public Bodies Order, 1946 is heavily laden with archaic control procedures and while it has admittedly been amended in some respects, it still forms the basis for the local authority accounting system. The demands of modern management have led local authorities to adapt their accounting systems to produce much more information for management purposes, facilitated by computerised expenditure systems. And this process is continuing.

5.23 But there needs to be a discernable modernisation of the system based on best accountancy practice. In particular, the system needs to be developed on full accrual and double entry accounting principles which give a better picture of the financial performance and true worth of the authority, both for management and for the general public. The system must also be developed to give more transparent information on the real cost of providing services.

5.24 It is therefore proposed to shift the emphasis from that of an accounting system to a financial management system to be developed in partnership with the local authorities. A project team has been set up to support and lead the process of designing and developing the new system, which will include:

- revising and modernising the existing legal basis underpinning the system;

- revising the basis of accounting, including accruals, asset valuation, balance sheets, year-end procedures etc;

- developing unambiguous accounting standards across all local authorities (including layout and content of each programme group etc), which will allow for standard methods of costing services;

- harmonising the work with that of the Local Government Computer Services Board in the computerisation elements of the new financial management system;

- rationalising the present arrangements for the provision by local authorities of various financial and statistical reports to central Government; ensuring that, where possible, financial reports should be generated directly by the computerised accounts system; and

- reviewing the role of the finance function in local authorities, to enable it to provide a strengthened, more professional role in the management of finances within local authority affairs; ensuring that a suitable training programme is available for staff to become familiar with all aspects of the new arrangements.

5.25 On a broader scale, in order to ensure optimum resource usage, better corporate planning is required within the framework of the SMI. This should involve the establishment of clear objectives for every programme, regular evaluation as to whether or not objectives are being realised and the adoption of new approaches when required. The potential use of information technology to underpin new approaches to work processes should be incorporated into the planning activities. Improved corporate planning will allow people and other resources to be deployed to best effect so as to achieve the objectives set for the services. Together with the use of modern project management techniques and IT-based monitoring and control systems, this will help to maximise efficiency of operations.

Value for money audits

5.26 Value for money auditing has been developing in the public service in the past five years. It shifts the focus of the traditional regulatory audit onto a broader view of the whole organisation and how it achieves its objectives. VFM is a relatively new activity for the Local Government Audit Service. Early studies undertaken by the unit were on comparatively defined areas (eg advertising, insurance); more recent studies have broadened into areas such as property management. While this VFM work is already proving beneficial it will be enhanced as follows -

- The role of the VFM Unit will be enlarged in terms of scope and application; with the experience gained from projects already completed, the unit will be in a position to undertake more comprehensive and more in-depth analysis of a wider range of local authority processes. The analysis will concentrate not only on the individual processes themselves, but also on how they interrelate to the overall workings of the local authority.

- As a special initiative, an efficiency audit will shortly be undertaken of county council operations in the roads area with a view to maximising efficiency. This will be completed within twelve months of commencement. This audit will be conducted by consultants appointed by the Department of the Taoiseach as part of the Government's efficiency drive under the SMI process.

- VFM concepts and practices will be introduced into the broader management training programme to be developed by the Local Government Management Services Board (LGMSB) referred to in chapter 6. This is to ensure that VFM is one of the core elements considered in any work process. This will underscore the fact that VFM is not an isolated concept to be considered as a separate entity to that of everyday work. It should permeate the activities of all managers and staff, to ensure that obtaining the best value from any operation is a primary consideration at all times.

- The VFM process will be supported through positive action:

  - training/development will be provided through the LGMSB for staff in areas identified by VFM studies as important;
  - networks will be set up between local authorities under the auspices of the LGMSB to share information and skills (eg materials management, energy management, etc); and
  - a specific officer will be designated in each local authority to ensure that VFM concepts are a focus of attention.

- The regulatory audit will be progressively re-focused to a VFM approach and will be underpinned with a legal status comparable with that of the Comptroller and Auditor General's role.

Financial performance indicators

5.27 It will be critical for the public service of the twenty first century to produce a top quality service using the most efficient deployment of resources. While there have been welcome improvements in efficiency over the years, the public service has not been driven by market considerations which tend to generate an efficiency imperative. The bottom-line profit motive is not likely to be a consideration for local authorities, but there will have to be much greater emphasis on producing quality outputs at competitive cost. Local authorities will have to be able to demonstrate to their customers (be they consumers or the tax-paying public) and to the private sector that they are cost effective organisations.

5.28 The new financial system to be developed will lay heavy emphasis on the costing principle. The system will be designed so that:

- it will be possible for each local authority to track the cost of producing each unit of service over time; and

- comparisons will be possible as between different local authorities.

A range of financial performance indicators will be generated and local authorities will be required to publish each year their performance against these indicators. The indicators will include the cost of providing specific services (eg cost of lifting a bin) and also other measures of the local authority's financial performance (eg debt collection performance). While these performance profiles will allow comparisons to be made between local authorities, their primary purpose will be to identify best practice and to encourage local authorities to improve their own performance levels. These measures will complement the measures proposed in chapter 4 for the development of performance indicators in the administrative/regulatory areas. A financial incentive scheme will be put in place under which awards will be made to local authorities which demonstrate particular innovations in reducing costs/increasing efficiencies (see para. 4.37).

Prompt payment

5.29 As part of a commitment to provide efficient services, local authorities will be subject to the provisions of the legislation being prepared on prompt payment by public sector organisations requiring them to settle invoices quickly.

Miscellaneous statutory levies

5.30 Local authorities have traditionally been required to make financial contributions to schemes over which they do not have control or which are otherwise outside their normal range of activities. Progress has been made over the past number of years in removing many of these statutory levies. Rationalisation of the current arrangements for coroners and veterinary services has begun and the remaining anomalies will be addressed in the near future.

Conclusion

5.31 The measures outlined above will ensure significant improvements in the funding available to local government. The programme of improvement of financial systems will lead to greater transparency in the financial affairs of local government. It will enable users of services and local taxpayers to form better judgements as to whether the local authority is delivering an efficient and cost effective service; it will be of considerable benefit to councillors in supporting their role in monitoring performance and in taking a strategic overview of local authority operations. And it will provide individual local authorities with an incentive to match best business practice.

Chapter 6 **Human Resources**

Introduction

6.1 The new focus and orientation for local government which the various proposals in this Programme aim at will be achieved only through full mobilisation of all of the resources of the local authorities. The most valuable resource is the 30,000 people employed in local authorities at a payroll cost of some IR£486 million, about thirty seven per cent of spending on current account. It is essential that this considerable asset is properly managed, motivated, involved and trained to deliver a cost-effective and quality service to the public.

6.2 The local authority personnel system has enormous strengths which are often taken for granted. Recruitment is objective and based on merit, the more senior positions being filled on the recommendation of an independent agency. All of the top management positions are filled by competitions open to all comers, though in practice most positions tend to be filled by people already in the system. There has traditionally been a high degree of mobility between local authorities in the administrative, professional and management grades which brings an infusion of fresh ideas to individual areas. The workforce conducts its affairs professionally and serves, with equal diligence, councils of different political complexions. And the service has a justifiably high reputation for accountability and probity in its stewardship of public funds. The system has delivered considerable productivity; the extensive range of additional responsibilities over the years has largely been accommodated within existing staffing complements. Numbers employed at the end of 1995, at just under 30,000, have not increased since 1989 and are some 5,000 less than the numbers employed in the early 1980s.

6.3 But there are weaknesses in the system which inhibit effectiveness -

- Traditionally, DOE has exercised extensive control over personnel matters, often extending to minor details.

- The management structure in local authorities is geared towards operational matters, but not so well geared towards policy development, including support for the councillors' policy role.

- The generally small size of local government units makes it difficult for individual local authorities to plan and implement developmental human resources policies.

- The multiplicity of clerical and administrative grades, the separate professional and administrative structures, and the separation of officer and non-officer streams create rigidities and a tendency towards hierarchical management practices.

- In the clerical and administrative stream, there is in practice very little open recruitment above the basic entry grades and recruitment practices at all levels are heavily circumscribed by regulation.

- Training tends to be ad-hoc, with a heavy emphasis on legal issues; it needs to be focused more on supporting the objectives of the system and to be based on planned training needs assessment.

- Participation rates by women in the higher administrative, engineering and management levels are widely acknowledged to be seriously deficient.

6.4 The paragraphs which follow set out proposals for modern and responsive human resources policies designed to deliver the renewal of local government envisaged in this Programme. There will be full consultation with staff interests before these proposals are implemented.

Central controls

6.5 It is crucial to the SMI process that individual units of the public service set their own goals and objectives - subject, of course, to overall resources and to public policies - and have the freedom and flexibility to manage their own affairs to fulfil those goals and objectives.

6.6 The unified local authority staffing arrangements developed from the 1940s onwards were based on a high degree of mobility for officer grades and standard conditions of service throughout the local government system. This standardisation was achieved through considerable central involvement and an extensive array of statutory consent procedures operated by DOE relating to pay, numbers, conditions of service, qualifications for appointments, recruitment procedures and so forth. These controls can have a dampening effect on local management initiative and lead to a culture of referral to central Government. It was for these reasons and in keeping with the SMI that a considerable proportion of the control apparatus applying in the human resources area was dismantled earlier this year. It is intended to continue this process and to devolve further human resources decisions to local authorities subject to the following principles -

- In common with all other public service organisations, local authorities will have to abide by Government policies on staff numbers and remuneration policies.

- Local authorities must continue to live within their budgets.

- Local authorities will have to act collectively in certain aspects of their human resources policies to ensure consistency and to avoid leap-frogging claims against individual authorities; arrangements for this are proposed below.

DOE's role will therefore shift in emphasis from control to co-ordinating local authorities' human resources policies in line with those of the Government.

New management system

6.7   The county management system is now well over fifty years old and the city management system even older. The role of manager, as envisaged when the system was established, is very different from what is needed as we approach the twenty first century. Not alone do local authorities have a significantly wider range of functions with consequent demands on the manager's time, managers are also expected to play a wider role in the affairs of the community generally and to take on many functions not directly related to the traditional core activities of the local authority.

6.8   Below the level of county manager and assistant manager, the management structure has not evolved with the changing role of local authorities and a proper policy development role has not been built-up. Some of this has to do with lack of resources, but much is due to inadequate structures. This has had an important effect on the development of the role of the councillor. The council is the policy-making arm of the local authority, but has not fulfilled this role as fully as the framers of the city and county management system intended. It is vital to the development of this role that proper support of a policy nature is given to the council and, in particular, to the new policy committee structure proposed in this Programme (see chapter 2).

6.9   There is an urgent need to strengthen the service at management level and to create a tier of management with clear and unambiguous responsibility for the programmes of the local authority. This programme manager approach will enable the necessary policy support to be provided for councillors under the new policy committee structure. It will also facilitate delegation of functions so that the city/county manager can become more concerned with strategic issues, and it will allow clear goals to be set for individual services and managers as part of the SMI process.

Strengthening the human resources function

6.10 The dismantling of departmental controls over human resources issues and the devolution of decisions to the local authorities will require a more active human resources management role by the local authorities. As most authorities are too small to maintain elaborate human resources management units, the further development of the human resources function calls for some services to be provided through co-operative action by local authorities acting collectively. It is proposed to establish, with effect from 1 January 1997, a Local Government Management Services Board (LGMSB) which will provide a comprehensive support system for the human resources function. The board will subsume the functions of the Local Government Staff Negotiations Board which primarily has an industrial relations focus. As the new board develops, it will be possible to further dismantle control mechanisms and to devolve further human resources functions from DOE in stages.

Partnership between staff of local authorities and DOE

6.11   The development of partnership is a key theme of this Programme - partnership between central and local authorities, between local government and local development organisations and between town and county authorities. The relationship between DOE and local authorities is a special form of partnership, bonded in strong common purpose and sharing the same objectives and strategies in many cases, albeit from different positions and with different perspectives. In the past year, this partnership has been deepened by the establishment of structured consultative procedures between DOE and the local authority associations at councillor level. There is a corresponding need to strengthen the consultative mechanisms between staff in DOE and local authorities. This will be achieved by having regular structured meetings between DOE staff dealing with specific programmes and a network of the appropriate local authority programme managers. These meetings will be in addition to the regular meetings which take place between the senior management of DOE and the county and city managers which will, in future, be more focused on issues at the strategic level.

Flexible work arrangements

6.12   The present grading arrangements in local authorities can give rise to rigidities and hierarchical methods of working. For example, local government personnel law differentiates between 'officers' (mainly the clerical, administrative, professional and technical grades) and non-officers who are, in law, still archaically termed 'servants'. The law originally conferred different tenures and superannuation arrangements on the two categories but many of the differences have been eroded over time with the development of labour law generally. However, there is little, if any, movement between the two streams. The current distinction between the streams is an anachronism which will be addressed in consultation with staff interests. In the meantime, it is proposed to make arrangements to permit a proportion of positions at the entry level in the officer stream to be filled by those wishing to progress, on merit, from the non-officer grades.

6.13   It is generally accepted that the present clerical and administrative grading structure contains too many grades for the average local authority. The restructuring package negotiated for these grades under the *Programme for Competitiveness and Work* will go some way to 'flattening' the structure by amalgamating the three lowest grades. But there is a case for looking for further rationalisation and this will be discussed with staff representatives as soon as possible. A flatter structure should enable more flexible working arrangements to be put in place.

6.14   The demarcation between town authority and county is dealt with in chapter 7. A unified staffing structure with full lateral mobility will be the aim; arrangements for implementation will be developed in consultation with relevant staff interests.

6.15   Local authorities employ a large number of professionally qualified and technical staff, mostly engineers. Engineers have a totally separate career path from recruitment level to county/city engineer and, with few exceptions, they have tended not to get involved in corporate management although many are, of course, managers of technical programmes and of staff. Thus we have the so-called dual structure. In many cases, the extreme features of this structure have been overcome by effective team work. Nonetheless, the existence of two different hierarchical structures where, effectively, the engineering structure is separate from key management decisions, continues to be a feature in many local authorities. The creation of a programme management tier should offer an opportunity for engineers and, indeed, other professional/technical staff, to get involved in corporate management and should ensure that more of them will aspire to the senior management positions in the local service.

Recruitment practices

6.16   Recruitment processes generally in the local government system, whether carried out by the local authorities themselves or by the Local Appointments Commission (LAC) have their origins in the 1920s. They were a response to the many haphazard and doubtful recruitment practices then existing. As might be expected, there is a heavy emphasis on fairness through regulation, rather than on best modern practice. While there has inevitably been some development of policy and practice over the years in response to circumstances, it is now time to carry out a general review of recruitment processes in the local government system to better reflect modern conditions and needs, while retaining the justifiable reputation for probity which the existing system has earned. This review will be put in hand immediately.

6.17   Current recruitment practices to clerical and administrative grades involve general entry at grade III level. There are limited opportunities at grade IV level, where fifty per cent of vacancies are filled by open competition. The entry qualifications for all of these positions are second level education. The effect of this, when taken with the fact that, in practice, the more senior grades of county secretary and upwards are mostly filled from within the system, is that there is practically no outside recruitment except at school leaver level. In the belief that the system would benefit from some outside recruitment at the intermediate levels, it is proposed to provide opportunities for graduate entry on the lines of the administrative officer grade in the civil service.

6.18   Contracts of employment were introduced for city and county manager posts in 1991 and the new arrangements have worked satisfactorily. The question of extending the contract system to other senior management posts (including professional/technical posts) will be considered. Local authorities already engage staff on short-term contracts to work on specific infrastructural projects. This practice could usefully be extended by engaging on short-term employment contracts, people who may be needed for other specific projects or assignments at other levels of the organisation, including clerical, administrative and management levels.

Development of staff resources

6.19 In responding in an effective manner to the policies outlined above and in other chapters of this Programme, significant changes will be required in the style and managerial competences at all levels of management. The quality of the leadership given by management at the strategic level will be a major factor in creating the environment for change and in mobilising for that change. Managers at all levels will have to become more aware of the critical success factors needed to achieve the results required. There has been a tendency in staff development programmes to concentrate on acquiring a detailed knowledge of the law and staff readily participate in these programmes as they are seen as a passport to advancement in the service. Local authorities can never forget that they must conform with procedures and the law in the conduct of their affairs. They must always take account of their obligations to protect the interests of the whole community and not just of the person who happens to be the customer at the moment. However, managers need to focus on results as well as on procedures and to develop the skills necessary to lead and motivate staff in this direction.

6.20 This will require more emphasis to be placed on team work, performance, networking, leading and motivating. In particular, the emphasis in the Programme on improving local authority performance in a measurable way using performance indicators and setting standards must carry through to the management of people. It is important that performance management systems are established which measure and appraise individual performance in a way which is linked with the objectives of the local authority. There will also be a need to orientate towards more effective policy support for the councillors through the new committee system proposed in chapter 2.

6.21 The development of these skills in managers at all levels will involve a considerable investment in management training and development if the objectives set out in this Programme are to be achieved. As well as developing management skills, there is a need for a structured programme of training and development for local authority staffs at all levels and in all disciplines; for example, training is required in individual programme areas, management and supervisory skills, interviewing skills, information technology, communications, dealing with the public, and health and safety. The assessment of training and development needs and the identification of suitable providers for this training and development will be a priority area for the LGMSB. It is generally accepted that investment in staff training should be at least three per cent of payroll cost and local authorities will be expected to meet this target within a reasonably short timeframe.

6.22 Mar a luadh i gcaibidil 4, tá na h-údaráis áitiúla tar éis a bheith an-ghníomhach maidir le bearta a chur chun cinn a chuireann ar chumas daoine a gcuid gnóthaí a dhéanamh as Gaeilge. Ach tá go leor acu i ndiaidh i bhfad níos mó ná seo a dhéanamh ó thaobh forbairt agus úsáid na teanga go laethúil i measc na foirne oibre, trí chúrsaí oiliúna a eagrú chomh maith le h-imeachtaí éagsúla sóisialta agus cultúrtha a chuireann deiseanna ar fáil leis an teanga a úsáid. Ní mór leanúint don spreagadh agus don tacaíocht atá á dtabhairt don ghealltanas seo i leith na Gaeilge agus chultúr na hÉireann. Maidir leis na h-údaráis áitiúla nach raibh gníomhach fós ina leith seo, beifear ag súil leis go réiteoidh siad cláir fheiliúnacha oibre dá bhfoirne agus go gcuirfear i bhfeidhm iad seo.

Women in local authorities

6.23   There is a clear gender imbalance in the management levels in the local authority service. There is no doubt that there are very many women in the service who possess the abilities necessary for management. This largely untapped source of management potential must be developed in order to ensure that the widest possible pool of talent is available in the future. The new management approach outlined above, with less emphasis on hierarchy and authority and more emphasis on team work and networking, may well attract more women to progress into management. To encourage this, a special development programme will be established for women managers. The programme will be specifically targeted at ensuring that a greater proportion of women are in a position to compete effectively for posts leading to management levels. The LGMSB will be asked to pursue this as a matter of urgency.

6.24   In the engineering profession, local authorities employ predominantly the civil engineering discipline. While there has been a welcome increase in the proportion of women graduates in this side of the profession in recent years, the proportion - at considerably less that one-fifth - is still low. As this improves, it will be expected that there will be an increase in the candidature of women for engineering positions in local authorities. For its part, the LAC will ensure representation of women on interview boards for engineering positions.

6.25   Indeed, there have been regular complaints about the lack of gender balance on interview boards, particularly at local level, and, while it has not been suggested that this of itself has resulted in gender imbalance in results, it is acknowledged to be unsatisfactory. The LAC has made considerable strides in ensuring that there is increasing participation of women on its interview boards - fifty four per cent of boards in 1995 and eighty two per cent in 1996 had women members. Local authorities are being asked to place considerably greater emphasis on this important aspect of recruitment policy too.

Community employment and other employment measures

6.26   Local authorities play a major role in supporting community development through sponsorship of a wide range of projects under the community employment programme, funded by FÁS. The projects are aimed at improving the local environment and developing heritage, tourism and leisure activities, and other community services which would otherwise not be available. Relevant local authorities are also participating in the Job Initiative (developed by FÁS to provide employment, on a term basis, for those who have had no regular employment in the last five years) which will operate in the area partnership areas in Dublin, Cork city, and Limerick city. Local authorities have been encouraged to build on their current input to the community employment programme by the inclusion of opportunities for training and employment of long-term unemployed persons in their action plans under OPLURD. In sponsoring these projects, local authorities provide work opportunities for the long-term unemployed and contribute to the economic and social well being of communities.

Employment of people with disabilities

6.27 In developing their human resources programmes, local authorities will be expected to play their full part in meeting the Government objective on the employment of people with disabilities to a minimum of three per cent of staff. While considerable progress has been made in recent years (the percentage overall is now 2.3 per cent), local authorities generally must make further efforts to at least meet the three per cent target and ensure that employment opportunities are offered to the fullest extent possible to persons with disabilities. Local authorities will also be expected to maximise opportunities for people with disabilities on contract and community employment work.. A code of practice is being developed by a working group to provide clear guidance in relation to this important issue. This is being prepared in consultation with staff interests and the National Rehabilitation Board.

Conclusion

6.28 The approach to human resources management in local authorities to date has been grounded on standardisation effected through central Government prescription and control. The new approach signalled in this Programme is based on local authorities having the freedom to manage their human resources, within budget, to deliver more effective services to the public. Managers and their councils will be able to find individual ways of working which suit the particular circumstances of their areas. Such diversity of approach will be welcomed and encouraged. Experiments are already being carried out in several local authorities on new ways of bringing services out into areas closer to the communities they serve. The one stop shop concept outlined in chapter 4 will require different deployment of staff resources. The further development and implementation of innovative approaches by local authorities to managing their resources will facilitate these developments.

Chapter 7 **Organisational Issues**

Introduction

7.1   The structure of local government is based on three levels -

- At regional level, eight regional authorities carry out the task of co-ordinating public services in the region and have monitoring and other functions in relation to the use of EU structural funds.

- At county/city level, thirty-four local authorities are the mainline providers of local government services.

- At sub-county level, eighty town authorities carry out local government functions - in some cases an extensive range of functions - in relation to the town; many county councils also operate through area committees and some are beginning to develop the provision of a range of services at this level.

In total, there are 114 elected local authorities (see statistical data in appendix 2). There are also over one hundred separate local development agencies (see appendix 3) which involve the social partners, community and State sectors. Proposals for closer integration of the two systems have been set out in chapter 3.

7.2   The general shape of the present local government structure was laid down almost a century ago, but important adjustments were made quite recently, with new arrangements for Dublin, the development of the regional tier, and the extension of town electoral boundaries for the 1994 town elections. Further structural change should be avoided at this point pending the introduction of the new funding system and the potential strengthening of the management and human resources dimension. However, there are some organisational issues which arise at this stage and which need to be dealt with.

The regional level

7.3   There is a great deal of public authority business conducted at the regional level. For many years, semi-autonomous regional bodies have operated in the health, tourism promotion and fisheries development areas; non statutory regional development organisations operated up to 1987; and proposals for regional education boards are well advanced. In addition, a considerable number of government departments and State agencies operate through regional offices; the Garda Síochána being the latest addition, with its new regional command structure. It was against this background that eight regional authorities were established on a statutory footing in 1994, with a specific mandate to promote co-ordination of public authority business at the regional level, and to monitor and advise on the implementation of EU funding in the regions.

7.4 The membership of the regional authorities consists of county/city councillors from the region who are appointed by the constituent local authorities. They are supported by an operational committee which includes the relevant county and city managers and executives of various public agencies. Additionally, for EU purposes, a wide range of interests is represented on a special monitoring committee. The regional authorities are funded by the constituent local authorities with special support provided by the Department of Finance in respect of EU related functions.

7.5 The regional authorities operate on a relatively modest scale; it was never the intention that they should have an invasive role in services delivered by others. The scale of their operations can be judged by their annual operating expenditure levels, which range from about IR£100,000 to IR£200,000 and their staffing levels which, typically, include the Secretary and generally one or two other employees. All regional authorities have now produced a regional report as they were required to do. On the basis of these reports and of contacts with the regional authorities, the following conclusions can be drawn -

- The principle of seeking to co-ordinate public service planning at the regional level is fundamentally right.

- The level of commitment from all public bodies, including the local authorities, to the work of the regional authorities needs to be substantially increased.

- Better systems for supporting the work of the regional authorities need to be developed.

- A range of specific tasks could be undertaken at regional level to underpin the broad planning role of the regional authorities.

- Regional boundaries may need to be reviewed in certain cases.

7.6 The following measures will therefore be taken to improve the capacity of the regional authorities to fulfil their mandate and strengthen their strategic planning role -

- In building up commitment to the regional concept, local authorities will be required to lead by example. They will need to have regard to the regional dimension as regards the provision and delivery of their services. They are themselves major providers of public services in the regions and many of these services spill over county/city boundaries. Aspects of water catchment management, and waste management services are examples. While these functions will remain with the primary local authorities, the regional authorities will become the focus for strategic planning for these services. The county/city managers of the local authorities will therefore be required jointly to prepare periodic reports, for submission to the regional authority, with specific proposals for co-ordinating local government services within the region.

- A county/city manager will be assigned overall responsibility for the regional authority to provide better co-ordination and linkage with local authorities (eg to help facilitate flexibility as regards staffing, assembly of project teams and local authority co-operation generally). The regional secretary, suitably retitled, will continue to have frontline responsibility in serving the authority.

- The other public bodies represented on the operational committees of the regional authorities will be required to make a modest financial contribution to the regional authorities, to improve their sense of 'ownership' of the regional authorities' policies and work, and to submit periodic reports of their activities in the region and of future plans.

- The Government has already decided that the Dublin and Mid-East Regional Authorities should play a role in drawing up strategic planning guidelines for the greater Dublin area. These guidelines will have to be respected by the constituent local authorities when adopting their five year development plans. The next Planning Act will give statutory backing to this process and will extend the arrangement to other regional authorities as necessary.

- The National Strategy on Sustainable Development, shortly to be published, will assign important and distinct new responsibilities to the regional authorities in the promotion of sustainable development; these will complement the strategic planning role of the authorities.

- There is a case for a review of the boundaries of some regional authorities based on patterns of settlement and transport and other strategic issues. The Border region and the Dublin and Mid-East regions are cases in point. These boundaries will be reviewed when planning for the next round of structural funds gets under way.

- The current arrangements are that the councillors, supported only by the Secretary, operate at the policy level, while the officers of the various public services function at the operational committee level; this may result in unduly rigid demarcation between councillors and officials. A fundamental review of current organisational arrangements will be carried out and implemented in the light of proposals for the next round of structural funds.

The county/city level

7.7   For local government purposes, the State is divided into twenty-nine county and five city areas, of equivalent status, each with a separate elected council. This framework is based closely on the twenty-six historical counties to which there are strong ties of local identity. The thirty-four county/city authorities are the primary units of local government and are responsible for the full range of local authority services; together they encompass the entire State. There are, in all, a total of 883 elected county/city councillors. These authorities range in population size from 25,000 to 481,000 - over one-third are under 60,000.

7.8 Many of the county units are too small to have a sufficiently diversified staff structure to deal with the full range of increasingly complex services for which they are responsible. Some services now demand a scale well beyond county level. At one extreme, some of the more complex environmental functions have moved to the national level with the establishment of the EPA. For others, the current operational context is now at inter-county or regional scale eg river catchment management. These trends are intensifying for other services like waste disposal.

7.9 In line with the established policy of governments over the years, the county/city level will remain the principal unit of local government. However, it will be necessary to encourage three specific trends -

- Firstly, for the services which have a significance beyond the county boundaries, greater co-operation between local authorities will have to be put in place. The proposals, outlined above, requiring the county/city managers concerned to produce joint policies/plans within the framework of the regional authorities should ensure a co-ordinated approach to these services. The particular services concerned will vary from area to area, depending on the size of the counties and topographical and other factors. Services receiving or likely to require this type of co-operative effort at the regional level include planning guidelines, waste management and lake and river catchment policies.

- Secondly, for most local authority services, the county and city level is reasonably suitable for planning and administration purposes. But local communities are demanding a greater say in the delivery of these services and more convenience in how they can avail of them. Some county councils have acknowledged this trend and have organised themselves on an area committee basis; others are planning comprehensive service delivery arrangements at the area level. Again, it is not possible to be over prescriptive in what arrangements should apply; the need for the area approach will clearly be greater in the larger, more dispersed counties. But as a general principle, local authorities will be encouraged to decentralise decision making and service delivery to their areas while taking due account of local circumstances.

- Thirdly, for areas adjacent to local authority boundaries - city/county; county/county; town/county - it will be necessary to critically review the organisation of local service delivery arrangements (including co-operation at member level in appropriate cases) to ensure that they are tailored to reflect actual realities. For example, the operation of entirely separate work teams rigidly adhering to administrative boundaries in what is a single urban centre is unlikely to maximise efficiency.

The sub-county/town level

7.10 At sub-county level some towns, but not all, have their own elected town authority. There are eighty town authorities (boroughs, urban district councils, towns with commissioners) which in total represent about fifteen per cent of the population of the State and have 744 councillors in all. Town authorities do not give a comprehensive territorial coverage and operate as isolated islands within the counties. In all towns, the county council provides services in respect of libraries, more complex environmental functions, generally for national and regional roads, fire and building control, etc.; in the smaller towns the county generally provides considerably more services. The range of functions actually carried out by the town authorities themselves varies considerably. In the larger towns, the range is extensive; in the smaller ones it is very narrow.

7.11 Each county and city is divided into local electoral areas - the councillors' constituency - for the purpose of electing councillors to the council. There are, in all, 177 local electoral areas at the county/city level; typically about five per local authority. Many county electoral areas are based on a town which also has its own separate elected town council. Town residents vote for both county and town councillors. In many towns outside the county town, there may also be a county council engineering or other office but generally such offices are not public access points. However, in a number of cases, some authorities are moving to expand the range of services provided by these offices.

Commission on town local government

7.12 Town local government was the subject of a report by a commission appointed under the Local Government Act, 1994 and representative of town, county and other interests. The report *Towards Cohesive Local Government - Town and County* was published in June 1996. The overall thrust of the report was to achieve greater cohesiveness in the delivery of services between town and county - and for customer service to be the central determinant in the way the town and county system is organised and operated. In particular, the report saw the need for unified staffing arrangements, with town assigned staff carrying out county council functions and vice versa. Similarly, a single development plan would be produced for the town and its environs and adopted by the town and county councils as relevant. Arrangements for periodic joint meetings of the town councils and county area committees would also encourage a unified approach to common problems. In general, the report saw the provision of major services, such as water and waste water facilities being consolidated at the county level, with the town council concentrating on town and community development measures. A town improvement programme generated in partnership with local interests and reflecting measures affecting the town whether by town, county or community was proposed to provide a focus for co-operation.

Town local government - actions proposed

7.13 Town local government fulfils, to an extent sometimes lacking at other levels, the local government principle of subsidiarity - of delivering services close to the communities it serves. And it has a proud record of achievement. It is proposed, therefore, to support the development of town authorities and to enhance their capacity to play the fullest role possible in local government affairs. Subject to this, the general thrust of the report on town local government is accepted. The following paragraphs set out the actions to be taken.

7.14 In 1997, a structured system of town/county meetings will be introduced so as to provide for closer co-operation between town councils on the one hand and county council area committees on the other. To underpin this move, and to help provide a focus for the work involved on an ongoing basis, a joint town improvement programme will be introduced to provide a co-ordinated plan of action by both authorities for measures affecting the town. A working group is being established to prepare for the implementation of these measures.

7.15 It is essential that the present fragmentation of service to the public as between county and town authorities is ended and replaced, as far as possible, by a joint single point of public contact. This would deliver a comprehensive integrated range of services to the customer and maximise administrative capabilities and resources. The organisation of services also needs review. For example, the town authorities have no input to, nor responsibility for, works on national or regional roads in the town; these are the responsibility of the county council. In many cases, the county council offices are in another town. At its most extreme, this can lead to separate work forces for minor matters like street cleaning. This is neither in the interests of economy nor of good service to the public. Even in county towns, the town authority and county council have separate offices, usually in different locations. Local authorities should, as part of their SMI processes, develop arrangements for harmonised provision of services. Over time, as new office campuses are being developed, services should be delivered from the one location; these services should include the wider public service on the one stop shop principle. As an interim step, county and town authorities will be required to make arrangements for the provision of services in towns on a harmonised basis.

7.16 Further measures to implement the recommendations contained in *Towards Cohesive Local Government - Town and County* are outlined in paragraph 7.23.

Local electoral areas

7.17 The proposals in this Programme for integrating local government and the local development bodies, and for developing better arrangements for customers will inevitably result in some decentralisation of county/city services to the area level. When the detailed results of the 1996 census become available next year, a review of local electoral areas will be carried out by an independent commission. This will also take account of proposals for decentralisation of county service delivery, of the proposed closer linkage between town and county authorities and the potential for greater synergy in this regard.

Local government boundaries

7.18 Almost all local authority boundaries were determined in the last century. Current county, city and town boundaries do not therefore provide what might be the optimum areas for service delivery, effectiveness and convenience, taking account of modern transport and settlement patterns. However, existing county/city structures are suitable for most local authority functions and will remain the primary units of local government. The historical counties themselves attract strong traditional loyalties. Particular anomalies tend to arise in situations where urban centres are divided by local authority boundaries. Boundary alteration can however have significant financial implications which must be borne in mind; rearrangement of territorial responsibilities between two public bodies cannot be allowed to result in excessive demands on the national taxpayer or on local ratepayers.

7.19   A specific anomaly arises in relation to some town boundaries. For the 1994 town elections, the electoral area of many towns was extended to encompass most of the census environs surrounding those towns. This was a recognition that a town and it's built-up environs need to be treated as a coherent unit. However, while the expanded boundaries applied for electoral purposes, the boundaries for operational purposes remained unchanged while the whole question of town government was being examined by the commission on town local government. The situation which now applies is that councillors elected partly by voters in the environs of towns have no operational responsibility for those environs. Boundary revision needs, however, to take account of local circumstances and to avoid undermining the capacity of the county as the primary unit of local government.

7.20   The prime concern at all times must be the effective organisation of services and convenient service to the public, to whom inter-organisational anomalies are simply a source of inconvenience. This calls for a flexible system where priority attaches to putting in place the most effective service arrangements rather than a rigid adherence to administrative boundaries. Resources, human or financial, should not be locked rigidly into what can be fragmented administrative compartments but need to be adapted to meet the real situation as it exists on the ground. The proposed one stop shop centres delivering a unified town/county service to the public should help greatly in this regard. Local authorities are being asked to prepare, before the end of 1997, a programme setting out clear steps they are taking to maximise efficiency through co-operative arrangements. Incentives will be available under the awards scheme for the more successful initiatives (see para. 4.37).

7.21   There will be circumstances where boundary alterations will be necessary in the best interests of good organisational arrangements. However, it is often difficult to get agreement between the parties when the boundary question is raised. Since September 1996, a new code of law dealing with local authority boundary alteration has come into operation. It provides a framework in which boundary proposals can be assessed and processed by the local authorities concerned taking account of all the relevant factors, including the financial implications, and with provision for independent review in appropriate cases. The new boundary code applies to all categories of local authorities. Given current anomalies at sub-county level, this allows for action to be put in train in appropriate cases by the authorities concerned.

Local government legislation

7.22 Much progress has been made in recent years in updating the specific legal codes relating to particular services (eg air, water, housing, roads, waste etc). A good start has also been made towards updating the general local government law with the Local Government Acts of 1991 and 1994. However, the fundamental legislative basis for existing county/city and sub-county authorities is outdated and scattered over various nineteenth century and other enactments. It is unduly complex and fragmented, often with different provisions applying to the different classes of local authorities - a classification system which itself is archaic and of little meaning to the public.

7.23 Comprehensive legislation will be prepared to provide in a convenient format a statutory basis for our local government system. It will be enacted to coincide with the centenary of the 1898 legislation which provides the basis for much of the present local government system. The legislation will:

- generally modernise and consolidate local government law and repeal outdated legislation;

- further reduce statutory controls in the human resources and other areas;

- apply the titles regional, county, city and town councils in place of the present terms which have little meaning for the citizen;

- provide improved roles for town councils which are now town commissioners; a range of discretionary functions will be available coupled with a mechanism to acquire specific additional functions depending on capacity;

- establish an office of mayor in all local government towns;

- for towns without a town local authority, set out criteria and procedures for the establishment of an authority subject to specified population thresholds;

- allow a local authority, either on its own initiative or in partnership with other local authorities or local groups, to introduce a community development contribution for a defined period to meet the specific costs of worthwhile local community projects;

- consolidate water and waste water services functions at county level with provision for special inter-county arrangements, where appropriate;

- allow for inter-authority arrangements applicable to all authorities for other appropriate services to be made locally with flexibility for local service arrangements to take account of local circumstances; and

- provide for the new committee structure and local development role outlined in this Programme.

Conclusion

7.24   The measures described in this chapter will substantially improve the functioning of the regional authorities and improve the co-ordination of public services at regional, county and sub-county/town levels. The capacity of town authorities for action on town improvement will be enhanced and there will be greater co-operation between county councils and town authorities through the development of joint town improvement programmes and the harmonised delivery of services in towns. This means better delivery of public services at all levels.

Summary of Key Actions

The following is a summary and a guide to the key actions set out in the Programme. The relevant paragraphs of the Programme are quoted in brackets.

Strengthening democracy

- The Government will support constitutional recognition of local government (2.7 to 2.9).

- Ireland will sign and ratify the European Charter of Local Self-Government (2.10 to 2.12).

- Local government will be represented on the National Economic and Social Council (2.13 and 2.14).

- There will be an enhanced role for the democratically-elected councillors:

  - as local government integrates with local development and assumes a greater role in relation to other public services delivered locally (3.8 to 3.13);
  - they will have a more significant role in the strategic management of their councils. This will be achieved through the mechanism of Strategic Policy Committees (SPCs), based on the main services of the council, to be established in county and city and the larger urban authorities (2.19 and 2.20);
  - the chairpersons of these committees, together with the chairperson of the council, will form a corporate policy group which will give increased focus to the policy role of councillors and link the work of the different SPCs (2.21); and
  - they will be given greater support to enable them to fulfil these new roles (2.26, 2.27 and 2.30, and 6.8 and 6.9).

- The partnership approach to national economic and social planning will be mirrored in the representation on the Strategic Policy Committees of local interests (eg industry, voluntary organisations, farmers, environmentalists) relevant to the committees' work (2.22 and 2.23).

- County councils will be encouraged to decentralise decision-making and service delivery by building on the existing area committee system (2.29).

Widening the role of local government

- The systems of local government and local development (LEADER, Partnerships, County Enterprise Boards) will be more closely linked through:

  - the appointment by each county and city authority of a director of community and enterprise development (3.10); and
  - the establishment of Community and Enterprise Groups which will include members (at least half) drawn from local development bodies (3.10).

- Community and Enterprise Groups will promote co-ordination between local government and local development. They will produce plans by end 1997 for the integration from January 2000 of local government and local development. Partnership and participation will remain central features in this process to build on the success of the local development initiatives (3.10 to 3.12).

- Personnel of State agencies will be available (to attend local authority meetings where necessary) to discuss the policies being pursued locally by their agencies (3.13).

- There will be greater liaison between the Gardaí and local authorities through structured consultation arrangements (3.13).

- The Devolution Commission will identify a range of additional functions suitable for assigning to local authorities (3.4).

Improving the quality of service

- There will be greater emphasis on providing quality services and on serving the needs of customers (4.7 and 4.8, and 4.15 to 4.18).

- Performance indicators will be used to measure and compare local authority activities in the delivery of key services and a special working group will be established to identify the key standards and indicators (4.19 to 4.21, and 5.27 and 5.28).

- High level local project teams will be established to develop within six months, proposals for one stop shop centres covering a wide range of public services to be implemented on a pilot basis (4.9 to 4.13).

- Local authorities will undertake quality initiatives to improve particular services (4.34 to 4.36).

- A quality awards scheme will be introduced to encourage local authority work in this area (4.37).

- A comprehensive list of public rights to information from local authorities will be published (4.25).

- The general public will be given a legal right to attend council meetings (4.24).

Paying for local government

- A new system of funding will be introduced (5.8).

- The full yield from motor taxation will become a dedicated local authority revenue source from 1 January, 1997. A proportion of this revenue will be used to finance an equalisation fund which will be established to ensure fair treatment of all local authorities and no reduction in resources for any local authority (5.8 to 5.11).

- Central Government will still set the rates of motor tax but, for 1998 and onwards, county and city authorities will have power to vary the national rates. The variation will not exceed six per cent and this will be limited in the first year (1998) to a maximum of three per cent. There will be no increase in motor tax in the interim (5.8).

- The rate support grant to local authorities will be discontinued (5.8).

- Charges for domestic water supply and sewerage facilities will be abolished with effect from 1 January 1997 (5.5 to 5.7).

- The new arrangements have two main advantages:

  - buoyancy, as local authorities will benefit on a continuous basis from growth in car ownership (5.8 to 5.11); and
  - discretion, as local authorities will be able, within reasonable limits, to raise additional revenue locally in accordance with local needs and priorities (5.8).

- Targets will be set for local authorities to reduce and eliminate their financial deficits (5.12).

- Proposals will be developed to allow for a local contribution for a defined period towards specific developmental projects or programmes (5.13).

- A major programme will be put in place to ensure maximum efficiency and effectiveness in local authorities:

  - more extensive value for money auditing (5.26);
  - greater use of performance indicators and services standards (4.19 to 4.21, and 5.27 and 5.28);
  - a new financial management system (5.22 to 5.25);
  - a comprehensive efficiency audit of county council operations in the roads area which will be undertaken shortly (5.26); and
  - legislation for prompt payment by local authorities (5.29).

The human dimension

- The 30,000 people employed by local government are its most valuable resource (6.1 to 6.3).

- Consultation with staff interests on human resources proposals will be essential (6.4).

- There will be further devolution of decisions on human resources issues from DOE to local authorities (6.5 and 6.6).

- A new management tier will be created in local authorities with clear responsibility for individual programmes and a leading role in servicing the Strategic Policy Committees (6.7 to 6.9).

- A Local Government Management Services Board will be established from 1 January 1997 to support human resources management in local authorities (6.10).

- A special development programme will be established with the aim of increasing the number of women at management and professional levels in local authorities (6.23 to 6.25).

- The distinction between officers and non-officers - archaically referred to as 'servants' - will be abolished (6.12).

- Further 'flattening' of clerical and administrative grading structures will be sought (6.13).

- A unified staffing structure will be the aim for town and county authorities (6.14).

- With the development of the new management structure, greater opportunities will exist for the involvement of engineering and professional/technical staff in the management of local authorities (6.15).

- Recruitment will be subject to a general review; greater opportunities will be provided for graduate entry to local government (6.16 and 6.17).

- More investment will be required in training and development; local authorities will be expected to devote at least three per cent of payroll to staff training and development (6.19 to 6.21).

- A code of practice will be developed in relation to the employment of people with disabilities. Local authorities are required to meet the three per cent employment target at least (6.27).

Getting the organisation right

- Measures are proposed to improve the level of commitment of public bodies (including local authorities) to the regional authorities (7.6).

- The Dublin and Mid-East regional authorities will be assigned a role in drawing up land use planning guidelines for the greater Dublin area which will have to be respected by the local authorities in the area when considering development plans. This will be extended to other areas as necessary (7.6).

- The regional authorities will be assigned new responsibilities for promoting sustainable development (7.6).

- The county and city authorities will remain the principal units of local government; but action is proposed to take account of services requiring co-operative efforts on a larger scale; to encourage decentralisation to area level and to address service delivery where boundaries intersect (7.7 to 7.9).

- The development of town authorities will be supported and their capacity enhanced to play the fullest role possible in local government affairs (7.13 to 7.16).

- There will be greater co-operation between county councils and town authorities with the provision of services in towns on a harmonised basis and co-ordinated plans of action (7.13 to 7.16).

- A review of local electoral areas will be carried out next year by an independent commission (7.17).

- A new code of law dealing with boundary alteration is now in operation (7.21).

- Local government law will be consolidated and modernised (7.22 and 7.23).

Part Two

LOCAL GOVERNMENT SERVICES

8.1   Local authorities provide an extensive range of services. By way of background this Part summarises some of the more significant developments which are under way or planned for the major service areas.

8.2   Over the years, local authorities and DOE have operated on the basis of a series of strategic plans relating to the major services. These have included the *Environmental Action Programme*, the operational programmes for transport and environmental services, *A Plan for Social Housing*, *Social Housing - The Way Ahead, Recycling for Ireland*, etc. These can be referred to for more in depth treatment of the relevant services.

8.3   Earlier this year, DOE's *Operational Strategy* outlined the application of the strategic management process in the Department and included a brief review of the specific objectives of each major service. In the light of government policy generally and DOE strategy, local authorities will now, as part of the SMI process, develop their own locally based objectives and strategies for the particular services.

THE ENVIRONMENT

8.4   The overall objective is to protect the environment by securing the provision of a range of infrastructural services (including water, waste water and solid waste) necessary for both environmental and development purposes, to maintain proper regulatory and monitoring systems for environmental protection and to promote and co-ordinate the adoption of sustainable policies in relation to the environment and development.

Environmental protection

8.5   Local authority functions relating to environmental protection include the provision of:

- drinking water, waste water treatment, solid waste management and litter prevention and control;

- adequate regulation and monitoring in relation to the environment, through the administration of legislation on air/water pollution and waste management; and

- information on, and promoting public awareness of, the environment.

8.6   The role of local authorities as environmental authorities is now shared with the EPA which provides support in their environmental authority/regulatory role. The EPA also has a monitoring and overseeing function in relation to the performance by local authorities of their environmental functions generally.

8.7   While the local dimension of environmental protection is important, there are other environmental requirements, particularly those deriving from EU obligations, for which national Government must take responsibility. It is necessary to ensure that these requirements are also taken into account at local level.

State of the environment

8.8   A comprehensive report, *State Of The Environment In Ireland*, was published by the EPA in early 1996. This concludes that the quality of Ireland's environment is generally good and compares favourably with most other EU member states. However, problematic trends are also identified as regards:

- a continued increase in slight to moderate pollution of inland waters;

- increasing air pollution from road transport; and

- increased waste generation, despite improvements in recycling performance.

The EPA report considers that solid waste, agriculture and the urban environment will need special attention in terms of environmental management in the coming years.

Water services

8.9   Considerable expansion of the water supply infrastructure took place during the 1970s and 1980s; this has greatly increased the country's stock of serviced land. Emphasis has been placed during the 1990s on remedying quality deficiencies in water services (in particular on providing adequate treatment of waste water discharges) and on conservation in the management of water supplies.

8.10   Most major water services schemes are now co-financed by the EU Cohesion Fund. This Fund is administered on a project basis and central Government authorities are accountable to the European Commission for detailed monitoring and reporting of projects. While central Government supervision will therefore have to be maintained in relation to major EU co-financed water projects, the same level of supervision should not apply to other schemes. In relation to these, the aim is to assign greater discretion and responsibility to local authorities, such as now operates, to some extent, for small water and sewerage schemes.

Waste management

8.11   Municipal waste management remains predominantly a local authority service, although an increasing share in its provision is being taken by the private sector. The landfill infrastructure is in need of extensive upgrading/rationalisation in view of more demanding national and EU environmental standards. Progress towards this objective is slow because of the weight of public objections to such proposed developments.

8.12   There is a national objective of diverting at least twenty per cent of municipal waste from landfill to recycling by the year 2000. Total recycling of municipal waste stood at some 7.8 per cent by 1995; this is mainly driven by the voluntary and private sectors. There will be increased reliance also on the private sector to deliver on the twenty-seven per cent recovery target (for the year 2002) for packaging waste, a target to which the Government is committed. But it is clear that local authorities will also need to develop greater involvement with recycling, in association with the voluntary and private sectors.

Environmental regulation and monitoring

8.13   Local authorities have in general responded flexibly and well to the greater demands placed on them by EU-derived requirements for environmental protection. For example, nearly 2000 water licences were in force at the end of 1995, during which year also some 3,700 investigations into water pollution were undertaken by local authorities and some 3,000 warnings or advice notices issued. However, it is also acknowledged that the environmental regulation of complex industrial and other processes, as well as the function of hazardous waste planning and management, will be more effectively carried out at national level. These functions have therefore been assigned to the EPA.

8.14 Because of their responsibility for the treatment of waste water and solid waste (see above), local authorities are however also potential polluters. There is provision (in the Environmental Protection Agency Act, 1992 and in the Waste Management Act, 1996 respectively) to make local authorities more transparently accountable for the proper environmental management and control of these activities. These arrangements which involve formal supervision by the EPA are now being activated.

8.15 Local authorities are empowered under various environmental enactments to adopt management plans; these are to provide an overall policy framework and guidance for the administration of, for example, water or air quality management and waste management. However, local authority environmental management plans have up to now had a limited impact. Water quality management plans have mainly been prepared between a number of local authorities and on a catchment basis. This approach has been reasonably effective; it is intended shortly to encourage local authorities to build further on it, by promoting a number of pilot projects in lake catchment management, based on a broader concept of sustainable development and a wider involvement of sectoral/ economic interests. The role of the regional authorities will be developed in the promotion of sustainable development.

8.16 There has been little uptake of air quality management plans; smoke control areas have however been established by regulation in the built-up areas of Dublin and Cork, with good results. All local authorities adopted general waste management plans under the Waste Management Regulations, 1979. But in general these plans took too much time to complete and they have not been of a quality to exert due influence on subsequent decisions by local authorities and other relevant actors. A revised and more detailed approach to local waste management planning is envisaged in the Waste Management Act, 1996. This will be actively promoted.

Environmental awareness

8.17 As regards information and public awareness, local authorities have been responding both to new statutory requirements in this area and to enhanced public interest in the environment. The Access to Information on the Environment Regulations, 1996 (which replaced similar 1993 regulations) oblige all relevant public bodies to provide public access to environmental information. Local authorities, as the main environmental authorities, have to deal with the majority of formal requests under the regulations.

8.18 The new provisions on access to information are pioneering ones in terms of Irish public administration. While the rate of complaints to the Ombudsman in relation to local authority handling of complaints has been significant, the new Regulations of 1996 and the greater experience now gained by local authorities of the new system should ensure an improved service to the public in future.

8.19 Local authorities have also been active in developing voluntary initiatives to promote better environmental information and awareness. Many local campaigns and other awareness raising activities have been promoted. Linkages have also been established with the environmental information service of DOE - ENFO. Environmental monitoring data (for example, in relation to bathing water quality) are being made more accessible to the public. Local authorities will be encouraged to implement pro-active approaches to providing information on the environment: this will better ensure the public support which is necessary for effective protection of the environment.

Sustainable development

8.20 *Agenda 21*, the major blueprint for sustainable development which was adopted at the 1992 UN Conference on Environment and Development, states that local authorities, 'as the level of government closest to the people, play a vital role in educating and mobilising the public around sustainable development'.

8.21 The *Local Agenda 21* process (guidelines for which were issued to local authorities by DOE in 1995) is an important means by which local authorities can promote sustainability in their areas with the involvement of local communities. It seeks to provide a framework for changes in attitudes and practices to help move society towards sustainable development. *Local Agenda 21* encourages a focus on conserving resources, minimising adverse impacts on the environment and on society and obtaining the maximum benefit in financial, social and environmental terms from the carrying out of local authority functions.

8.22 Local authorities can promote sustainable development in three ways. First, they must integrate sustainability considerations into their own functions and policies, for example as planning, housing and roads/traffic management authorities. Secondly, local authorities must lead by example in 'greening' their own operations and performance through, for example, the application of green housekeeping and environmental management systems. Thirdly, local authorities can exercise a role of leadership, education and facilitation vis-á-vis the wider community, including business/industry and voluntary/NGO interests, so as to promote sustainable development. As set out in this Programme the introduction of the partnership model via the SPC system and enhanced roles for the regional authorities will serve to support local authority work in this area.

Actions

8.23 The following measures are under way or planned -

1. A major programme of investment is being implemented in the provision of water and waste water infrastructure to meet the requirements of EU Directives in relation to drinking water quality and waste water treatment.

2. Water conservation policies will be actively promoted in co-operation with local authorities.

3. Except for the major water and waste water projects being co-funded under the EU Cohesion and Structural Funds, a more devolved approach will be sought to the funding of water and waste water projects whereby local authorities will decide priorities as between the various schemes in their own areas within a system of block grants allocated by DOE on a three-year rolling basis. The existing small schemes sub-programme offers a useful precedent for this policy.

4. There will be an increased emphasis on the provision of support and training services to improve the management and maintenance of water services, with particular focus on front-line personnel.

5. Local authorities will have to ensure that in accordance with the polluter pays principle, industrial and commercial users of water and waste water services make an equitable contribution to the capital and operating costs of these services.

6. Responsiblity for water and waste water services will be consolidated at county/city level.

7. Local authorities will need to upgrade and rationalise the network of local authority landfills.

8. In co-operation with the private and voluntary sectors, local authorities will be requested to work to double the level of recycling of municipal waste by the year 2000, and in particular to attain national and EU targets for increased recycling of packaging waste.

9. Local authorities will be requested to intensify and improve their environmental performance, in particular under guidance being developed by the EPA.

10. The operation of environmental quality management plans by local authorities will be improved.

11. Local authorities will be requested to develop information policy statements as a commitment to openness and transparency in providing environmental information, to make local authority monitoring data more accessible and user-friendly, and to continue to promote environmental awareness activities and campaigns, where appropriate on a joint basis with community/NGO interests.

12. Local authorities will be requested to intensify action to accelerate the adoption of *Local Agenda 21* programmes and to seek more systematically to develop joint action and partnerships with other interests, including the business and farming communities and the voluntary sector, in promoting sustainable development.

13. A major initiative is underway to tackle the litter problem. The Litter Polution Bill, 1996 is one of series of measures to support action by local authorities.

DEVELOPMENT AND PLANNING

8.24 The overall objective is to promote the sustainable development of urban and rural areas in a manner which facilitates long term economic and social progress.

The planning system

8.25 Since 1963, local authorities have been responsible for securing a high quality natural and built environment through the control of development in their areas and by setting development objectives in the statutory development plan. The planning system is thus the primary mechanism for the proper planning and development of cities, towns and rural areas, with public consultation as a central feature. Modifications to the system since its establishment have expanded and underlined its openness and transparency.

8.26 Through the development plan process, comprehensive guidelines should be established every five years to underpin the provision of infrastructural services by the local authorities themselves and to inform development control policies. The process involves considerable public consultative arrangements. However, over time, the development plans have become overly elaborate, making it difficult for members of the public to relate to them. This can be a particular problem in the larger more rapidly developing local authority areas where the development plan process not only needs to comprehend the whole area but also to provide a more detailed focus with specific local action plans. The general policies proposed in this Programme concerning partnership and locality-based administration will call for some re-think in local authorities on how effectively their development plans represent community concerns about development of their areas, balanced against broader authority-wide issues and the overall common good.

8.27 Local authorities processed over 45,000 planning applications last year. The number of applications has been rising, reflecting economic performance. Some nine per cent of the total number of local authority planning decisions in 1995 were refusals of permission and some seven per cent of all decisions were appealed to An Bord Pleanála. Since 1992 there has been a major improvement in the speed with which An Bord Pleanála decides appeals; in 1995, ninety-eight per cent of appeals were decided within four months. The performance of local authorities in meeting their statutory target of two months for deciding applications varies considerably. On average, in 1995, seventy per cent of applications were dealt with within two months.

Urban renewal

8.28 The past decade has seen a major new emphasis on urban renewal polices. The key impetus has been the tax-based incentives introduced from 1986 and targeted at run-down urban areas. The tax incentives have been supplemented by specific initiatives, run by development agencies, aimed at regenerating specific areas such as the Custom House Docks and Temple Bar. More recently, under the urban and village renewal sub-programme of OPLURD, the URBAN initiative, and the *Special Support Programme for Peace and Reconciliation in Northern Ireland and the Border Counties of Ireland*, a system of grant support, based on area action plans, has been introduced. Local authorities have a major role in all of these initiatives which have transformed cities and towns.

Building control

8.29 Local authorities are also involved in the regulation of building standards through the Building Regulations. The Regulations generally operate on a self-regulatory basis subject to random checks by the authorities. However, prior approval must be obtained from local authorities in respect of the fire safety standards of new and reconstructed buildings other than dwellings.

Actions

8.30 The following measures are under way or planned -

1. The National Strategy on Sustainable Development, shortly to be published, will be developing proposals for building sustainability principles into development plans; land use planning guidelines on forestry development and high amenity land will be the next in a series of such guidelines which have included telecommunications antennae and support structures and windfarm development; and guidance notes on the scope and context of development plans will also be issued.

2. Regional authorities will be assigned a role in setting out stategic planning guidelines to be respected by the constituent local authorities in drawing up their development plans. This process will start with the Dublin and Mid-East Regions.

3. Local authorities will be encouraged to make greater use of their powers to make local area action plans; this will be essential in the urban renewal/local development context.

4. New legislation will be introduced to strengthen the powers and responsibilities of local authorities in relation to the protection of the architectural heritage, eg listed buildings, streetscapes etc. A comprehensive series of booklets giving advice on conservation of buildings has recently been published by DOE. It is intended that future urban renewal policies will support and promote the conservation of the architectural heritage.

5. In the period 1994 to 1999, expenditure of IR£80 million is scheduled for a range of physical improvements under the urban and village renewal sub-programme of OPLURD to promote economic and social development at local level. The main elements of this programme include major integrated urban renewal action plans in the five main cities and a range of urban and village improvement schemes throughout the country.

6. A consultant's report on the overall effects in economic, social and architectural terms of the urban renewal tax incentive scheme as it has operated to date has just been published. The report focuses on the role of local authorities and in particular on the formulation of a planned approach to urban renewal. This report will inform future policies on urban renewal which are currently under review. It can be envisaged that local authorities will have a central role in implementing more targeted and integrated urban renewal policies.

7. The tidy towns competition has recently been revamped to incorporate wider environmental considerations in relation to the built and natural environment in cities, towns and villages. Tidy towns committees are now encouraged to plan their activities and to co-ordinate their plans with other relevant local organisations, particularly local authorities. Local authorities can go a long way towards ensuring that the potential of tidy towns committees, in areas such as ensuring appropriate treatment of derelict sites and open spaces, provision of recycling facilities and the development of amenities, is fully realised by providing them with advice and other practical supports. The tidy towns movement has for many years shown the strengths of partnership between local authorities and local communities which will be extended on a broader front by this Programme.

8. A complete new set of technical guidance documents to underpin the Building Regulations will shortly be finalised; these will provide for enhanced thermal efficiency in buildings and will allow for sensitive application of the structural and fire requirements in the case of older buildings. Measures to improve local authorities' capacity to enforce the regulations are also being developed.

ROAD TRANSPORTATION

8.31 The overall objective of roads policy is to provide, within the framework of a balanced and integrated transport policy, for the safe efficient and cost-effective movement of persons and goods by road.

8.32 Local authorities play a key role in all aspects of road transportation including the improvement and maintenance of the public road network.

8.33 The modern road network now being put in place by local authorities, including national roads in association with the National Roads Authority, is providing essential infrastructural support for the development of the productive sectors of the economy and the creation of long-term sustainable employment. This is being achieved with considerable EU financial assistance.

8.34 Roads are the dominant mode of inland transport in the State both in relation to freight and passenger movements. This is because of Ireland's island status without permanent physical links to our trading partners, low density population, economic settlement patterns and our relatively short average journey length.

8.35 National roads, accounting for about six per cent of the 96,000km of public roads, are the major long distance through routes linking the principal ports and airports, cities and large towns, serving major geographical regions and a high proportion of the total population. The bulk of EU assisted investment will be in the national road network which carries about thirty-eight per cent of total road traffic. Over two-thirds of all journeys are work related and some one-sixth of these are by heavy commercial vehicles.

8.36 The extensive regional and county road system has come under severe pressure in recent years because of inadequate pavement structure or surface conditions of about thirty per cent of these roads due mainly to increased traffic volumes and vehicle weights. This has led to a major expansion this year of the special restoration programme for regional and county roads. It is intended that this programme will restore the regional and county roads throughout the country to a satisfactory condition.

Actions

8.37 The following measures are under way or planned -

1. The *Operational Programme for Transport*, which was agreed between the Government and the European Commission, provides the framework for investment in the network of national roads in the years 1994-99. Over the period, over IR£1.2 billion is being invested in improving the standard of the national roads network. The major underlying goal for this level of investment is to help Irish enterprise and underpin employment, by bringing the network up to the level where it can fully serve a vibrant expanding economy. Most of this funding is

going to four strategic corridors which link the major cities and centres of industry and carry the highest levels of traffic, both commercial and private.

2. As part of the non-national roads restoration programme, each county council has prepared a multi-annual road works programme for the years 1996 - 2000. Over IR£73 million is being spent on this programme in 1996. A study is at present under way which will definitively establish the extent and the cost of dealing with the backlog of deficiencies in the regional and local road network. This study will be completed by the end of February 1997.

3. An audit will shortly be undertaken of county council road construction and maintenance operations. This audit will be conducted by consultants appointed by the Department of the Taoiseach as part of the Government's efficiency drive under the SMI process. It is expected that this audit will be completed within twelve months of initiation.

4. A manual covering all aspects of road signage has just been published. It provides a comprehensive guide to all aspects of traffic signing and sets out the technical and other standards to be followed. New regulations governing regulatory signs will be made shortly.

5. The role of local authorities in traffic management has been considerably enhanced in recent years with the devolution of a number of powers and functions. These include the making of speed limit bye-laws and greater responsibility in the application of traffic management and traffic-calming measures. Comprehensive new traffic regulations will be made shortly which will greatly streamline existing arrangements which involve local authorities, the Gardaí and the Minister; this will further enhance the role of local authorities as the primary authority for the management of traffic in their areas.

6. Since September 1995 local authorities have been involved in the licensing of taxis and hackneys. All the major policy decisions are now vested in the councillors, and authorities have maximum discretion in relation to the development of taxi and hackney services in their areas. There will be continuing consultation with local authorities on the review of the operation and application of the legal framework governing their role in the provision of taxi and hackney services.

7. Local authorities collect motor tax in respect of cars, trucks and other mechanically propelled vehicles used in public places. They also issue driving licences and trailer licences and collect the fees payable. Proposals are being developed for a new computer system in motor tax offices which will streamline the procedures and improve the administration generally.

8. There will be increased emphasis on involving local committees, through their local authorities, in road safety programmes. As part of the *National Road Safety Together* strategy, local authorities will lead local working groups comprising engineers, road safety officers, Gardaí, teachers, etc to co-ordinate and enhance road safety efforts at local level.

HOUSING

8.38 The overall aim of housing policy is to enable every household to have available an affordable dwelling of good quality, suited to its needs, in a good environment, and as far as possible, at the tenure of its choice. The general strategy for realising the overall policy aim is that those who can afford to do so should provide housing for themselves with the aid of the financial incentives available, and those unable to do so from their own resources should have access to social housing or to income support to meet their housing costs.

8.39 Local authorities have for many years been the primary agents for the delivery of social housing to meet the needs of their areas. Almost one-third of the total occupied housing stock of one million dwellings was provided originally as local authority accommodation. Successive tenant purchase schemes have, however, enabled many former local authority tenants to acquire their houses. The current rented housing stock of local authorities stands at about 100,000 dwellings, housing some 350,000 people.

8.40 In recent years, the way in which local authorities deliver social housing services has changed significantly in response to changing demands and patterns of social housing need. New strategies contained in *A Plan for Social Housing* (1991) and *Social Housing - The Way Ahead* (1995) are strongly customer-centred with special emphasis on greater choice and higher quality social housing provision and management. Societal changes, high unemployment rates on local authority estates, increased crime and anti-social behaviour, much of it drug related, present new challenges to local authorities in their housing management function. These challenges go beyond the traditional local authority housing role and require new approaches, skills and resources.

8.41 The current housing programme meets the needs of some 10,000 households each year. The capital available for social housing provision in 1996 exceeds IR£260 million. Within this overall programme, local authorities will increasingly develop their promotional and facilitating role in housing, in order to improve and speed up access to housing for those in need. This will involve utilisation and co-ordination of the full range of social housing options including local authority housing, voluntary housing, shared ownership and other schemes.

8.42 The quality and management of the existing local authority rented housing stock is a key factor in the quality of life of tenants of local authority housing. Substantial progress has been made in improving the physical condition of the local authority rented housing stock. Local authorities will continue to improve their rented housing stock through housing refurbishment under the remedial works programme and through the provision of bathrooms for dwellings without such facilities under the bathrooms sub-programme, and other appropriate measures.

8.43 Local authorities have assisted in the provision of a significant increase in accommodation for homeless persons over recent years and have improved liaison with health boards and voluntary bodies. They continue to increase the supply of accommodation and improve co-ordination and delivery of services in response to the accommodation needs of homeless people.

8.44 In recent years, the responsibilities of local authorities in the area of private rented accommodation have been extended, particularly with regard to registration, rent books and standards. The objective is to help improve conditions and raise standards generally in the private rented sector and recent regulations are intended to provide information and resources to local authorities to assist their enforcement of the statutory requirements in this area in the coming years.

Actions

8.45 The following measures are under way or planned -

1. Local authorities will significantly develop their housing management responsibilities to deliver a high quality, cost-effective customer service. This will be facilitated by the work of the Housing Management Group, established by DOE, and recently strengthened by the appointment to it of representatives of the Department of the Taoiseach and Area Development Management Ltd., coupled with the setting up of new local arrangements between local authorities, partnership companies and local community groups. Development of the local authority estate management function will include greater tenant and community participation in the management of their estates, improved training for local authority housing staff and better information services in the housing area.

2. New legislation will provide additional powers to local authorities to deal effectively with serious anti-social behaviour in their housing estates, focusing especially on drug-related activity.

3. Further progress will be made in mitigating the extent and effects of social segregation in housing, particularly by way of smaller local authority housing estates and the use of infill sites to enable integration with existing services and communities.

4. New legislation will support the *National Strategy for Traveller Accommodation* and the adoption of five year traveller accommodation programmes by local authorities in consultation with local traveller interests and local community groups.

5. The major issues involved in transferring the administration of rent and mortgage supplementation (currently administered by health boards under the Supplementary Welfare Allowances scheme) to local authorities are currently being examined by an Inter-Departmental Committee, under the aegis of DOE and with representatives of the Departments of Finance, Health and Social Welfare.

FIRE, AMENITY AND OTHER SERVICES

Fire services

8.46 The functions of the fire authorities include making provision for extinguishing fires and dealing with other emergency incidents, including those arising from spillage of hazardous substances etc. Fire prevention functions include advisory and regulatory functions in relation to new and existing buildings. There are 217 fire stations throughout the country with over 3,000 fire service personnel of whom 1,200 are wholetime and 1,800 retained (part-time). Operationally, the diversity of the situations dealt with by the fire service has increased - transport accidents, hazardous materials, pollution incidents, rescues from various situations etc. The fire service is now generally the first line response to a variety of emergencies. In recent years there has been an increased emphasis on fire safety aspects which include design of buildings, fire safety education and fire prevention.

8.47 The Fire Services Council operates a central programme of courses for fire officers. Training is adapted to take account of changing needs such as transport accidents and incidents involving hazardous materials. The Council's annual training programme will continue to complement and supplement the training provided by local authorities.

8.48 All the main local authorities have plans to deal with major emergencies. An all-hazards approach to emergency planning is adopted, reflecting the many common features of emergency response. The Major Emergency Plan is implemented by the three main response agencies, ie the local authorities, the Gardaí and the health boards, each of whom have their own specific functions. Advice and guidance will continue to be provided to local authorities in relation to their emergency response role.

Actions

8.49 The following measures are under way or planned -

1. A good communications and mobilisation infrastructure is essential for the fire service. A modern computerised communications and mobilisation project (CAMP) is being implemented at present on a regional basis. Funding is provided by DOE. The project will provide a better service for the public when they need emergency services and the fire service will be better placed to respond to such calls.

2. Since 1981 well over IR£80 million has been provided from State funds to finance new fire stations, the purchase of fire appliances and emergency equipment, and improvements in communications. Capital investment will be maintained to meet the continuing needs of the fire service.

The public library service and local archives

8.50 The role of libraries continues to evolve. The library service now acts as an information and educational resource, runs programmes of out-reach activities and participates in partnerships with other groups. The public library service employs more than 1,300 people in over 300 branches. Current expenditure by library authorities in 1996 is estimated to be IR£32.5 million. Investment by DOE in 1996 in the development of public library infrastructure and the establishment of local authority archives services is IR£3 million capital and IR£0.6 million current expenditure.

Actions

8.51 The following measures are under way or planned -

1. In line with the evolving role and activities of the library service, DOE is currently preparing to initiate a library policy review. The objective of the review is to modernise the policy framework at national level for the development of the public library service.

2. Each local authority is now in the process of establishing a local archives service. This will be done in two phases. In phase I, local authorities will retain, manage, preserve and restore their archives. In phase II, they will put in place arrangements for public access to archives.

3. To assist the establishment and development of local archives services, DOE will issue to local authorities detailed technical guidelines, covering the issues related to the establishment and management of a local service. The DOE is also prepared to subsidise the salaries of qualified archivists engaged jointly by local authorities on a regional basis to establish or develop local archives services.

The arts

8.52 In recent years, local authorities have expanded considerably their role in the arts in the context of overall arts policy as developed by the Department of Arts, Culture and the Gaeltacht. Most of the major local authorities now employ an Arts Officer. Local authorities are recognised by the Arts Council as having a major role in the development of the arts in Ireland. Examples of local authority support actions include: provision of public sculpture, municipal galleries and art collections, support for locally-based publishers, organisation of readings and workshops, financial support of theatre and film festivals, publications on literary and artistic subjects, provision of theatre-in-education, grants to local art groups and support for professional touring companies. They also operate the per cent for art scheme whereby art works are commissioned as part of major infrastructural projects. Current expenditure by local authorities on the arts in 1996 is estimated to be in excess of IR£3 million. In addition, local authorities provide 'hidden' supports to the arts through the provision of venues, rates relief, staff time etc.

Actions

8.53　The following measures are under way or planned -

1. A review of the per cent for art scheme, with a view to diversifying the scheme and increasing its impact, is nearing completion.

2. Local authorities will play a major role in *The Arts Plan*, which sets out a coherent set of measures to spread the development of the arts to all parts of the country; the new funding arrangements provided for in this Programme will enable local authorities to mount a better support framework for the development of the arts.

Parks, recreational areas and swimming pools

8.54　The provision and maintenance of parks, recreational areas, and sports facilities has been carried out by local authorities for many years and demand continues to grow with rising living standards and increasing leisure time. Swimming pools for which DOE allocates grant aid are provided and refurbished by local authorities or by voluntary bodies in co-operation with them.

Actions

8.55　The future provision and funding of amenity/recreational/sports facilities, including swimming pools, is being examined in the context of the National Sports Strategy being developed by the Sports Strategy Group established by the Department of Education. The report of the Group is due for completion by the end of the year and this is expected to lead to better co-ordination arrangements among government departments, local authorities and Bord Fáilte, in the planning and funding of amenities/recreational facilities, including, in particular, swimming pools.

Introduction

1. There are 114 directly elected local authorities in five legal classes as follows -

    See map of local authority areas page 119

Class of Authority	Number of Local Authorities	Membership Range
County Councils	29	20-48
County Borough (City) Corporations	5	15-52
Borough Corporations	5	12
Urban District Councils	49	9-12
Town Commissioners	26	9
Total	**114**	**1,627**

They are responsible for an extensive range of services which are outlined below. While the general shape of the local government structure was laid down almost a century ago, there have been important adjustments recently with the establishment of three new councils for Dublin in 1994 and the setting up of eight regional authorities (see paragraph 23 below) in the same year.

Local authority functions

2. Local authorities are multi-purpose bodies which operate subject to statute law. In addition to the general law relating to the local government system, specific codes apply to different services - eg Planning; Roads; Housing; Sanitary Services; Water Pollution; Control of Dogs; Fire Services; Motor Tax, etc. The functions of local authorities are classified into eight programme groups as follows -

    (i) **Housing and Building**

    Assessments of housing needs; provision of housing to meet those needs, either directly or through social housing initiatives; collecting rents; housing management and maintenance services (including tenant participation); assistance to people housing themselves or improving their houses; enforcing certain housing standards and registration of private rented sector; and accommodation of travellers and homeless persons.

    (ii) **Road Transportation and Safety**

    Upkeep and maintenance of roads; public lighting; traffic management; car parks; road safety promotion; registration and collection of motor vehicle taxation; licensing of drivers; and licensing of taxis and hackneys.

(iii) Water Supply and Sewerage

Operation and maintenance of public water supply and sewerage schemes; the provision of services to households, commercial and industrial users; and assisting private water schemes.

(iv) Development Incentives and Controls

Preparation and making of development plans; deciding on planning applications; enforcement action; urban renewal; building control; promotional activities in the areas of tourism and industrial development; and other community development activity.

(v) Environmental Protection

Preparation of air and water quality and waste management plans; monitoring and enforcement of pollution controls; deciding on licencing applications; operation and maintenance of landfill sites; collection and disposal of waste and refuse; operation and maintenance of burial grounds; civil defence; dangerous buildings; water safety; fire fighting and fire prevention; and street cleaning and litter prevention.

(vi) Recreation and Amenity

Operation and maintenance of a range of amenities such as swimming pools, libraries, parks, open spaces, community centres, galleries, museums, recreation centres and such like.

(vii) Agriculture, Education, Health and Welfare

Payment of higher education grants; contributions to VECs; payment of VEC pensions; aspects of animal disease control and land drainage; and some minor involvement in services of a social/educational nature.

(viii) Miscellaneous Services

Rate collection; elections; courthouse maintenance; coroners and inquests; malicious injury claims; operation of markets; abattoirs; dog control; and general administration.

The county/city authorities are required to produce an annual report on the performance of their functions.

3.   The full range of the above functions are legally vested in the county/city authorities, which are the primary units of local government. While the urban authorities (five borough corporations and forty nine UDCs) have a fairly extensive range of functions, they are not responsible for the full range shown above. Some functions are carried out by county councils throughout the entire county - including the urban areas. For example, motor tax, library and generally national and regional roads, fire, building control, emergency planning and most aspects of pollution control are the responsibility of the county council in all areas. The main difference between boroughs and urban district councils is mainly historical; they exercise largely the same functions. In some cases, functions which are legally vested in urban authorities are exercised on their behalf by the county council on foot of local agreements. The

functions of town commissioners, which exercise a mainly representational role, are much more limited than those of the other classes of local authority; most functions in those towns being vested in the county council.

4. While overall local government structures have not significantly changed, functional responsibilities have been extensively adapted - for example, new local authority roles have grown in areas such as environment, planning, urban renewal, housing and general development while health functions have moved to the regional health boards established in 1971. In recent years, the EPA and the NRA have been established to support and assist local authority environmental protection services and national road services, respectively.

The elected council

5. Councillors constitute the elected council of a local authority and occupy the pre-eminent position in the authority (see paragraph 10 below). They are elected for a five year term under a system of proportional representation. For the purposes of elections, the local authority area for the county/city and some larger urban authorities is generally divided into a number of multi-seat local electoral areas. For councillors, these areas are the equivalent of Dáil constituencies. There are several prohibitions on holding membership of a local authority. Some of these reflect its distinctive nature, by limiting the extent of the dual mandate (eg Ministers and Ministers of State are disqualified). Additionally, after the next local elections certain other Oireachtas office holders and MEPs will be added to the list. Oireachtas members will also then be disqualified from holding the position of local authority cathaoirleach or leas-chathaoirleach.

6. Generally, most local authorities hold monthly meetings, although some meet more frequently. Most of the county/city councils and the larger urban authorities also operate a number of separate committees. The smaller urban authorities make more limited use of committees. Such committees generally deal with specific matters such as housing, roads, planning etc; some city/county authorities also operate a system of area committees based on local electoral areas. Decisions are made by councillors at meetings of the local authority and its committees and are reached by consensus or majority vote. Each local authority elects a chairperson (cathaoirleach) or mayor annually from among its members.

7. Almost all councillors are part-time. Because of the part-time nature of the work, councillors do not receive a salary. However, they receive an annual allowance designed to cover travel and subsistence expenses as well as an element relating to representational expenses. Chairpersons are also paid an allowance.

Representational role

8. In addition to the specific statutory functions outlined in paragraph 2 above, a fundamental role of democratically elected local government is representation of local communities, voicing local concerns and responding to local needs. Councillors represent their electorates over a range of

public issues and would thus have a concern with, for example, the operation of other public agencies within their area and with the general development of the area. Local authorities also have a right of representation on a range of other public agencies which operate locally such as health boards, VECs and harbour boards.

Council and executive

9. The elected council is the policy making arm of the local authority while the day to day management is vested in a full-time salaried chief executive - the city/county manager. Legally all functions, whether performed by the elected council or the city/county manager, are exercised on behalf of the local authority.

10. The councillors exercise what are termed 'reserved functions' defined by law, and specified across a whole range of enactments. These comprise mainly decisions on important matters of policy and finance (eg adoption of annual budget, development plan, waste management plan, scheme of letting priorities). The general policy role of councillors is explicitly recognised in local government law as is the right of members to represent the views of the local community to other public bodies. The manager discharges what are termed 'executive functions' - in effect the day to day running of the authority - within the policy parameters determined by the councillors. Apart from the policy role, as expressed via the different reserved functions, the elected council, in addition, has various powers in relation to the operation of the executive role. These allow for oversight and direction of the affairs of the authority generally, and for directing the manager in the performance of the executive role in certain circumstances. The manager has a duty to advise, and assist, the councillors in the exercise of their functions and can attend and speak, but not vote, at meetings. While the division of functions between councillors and the manager is clearly defined for legal purposes, in practice, the policy and executive roles are not wholly divorced and the councillors and manager operate together, with the former intended to have the pre-eminent role.

11. The county/city manager who is an officer of, and employed by, the county/city authority, is effectively recruited by the Local Appointments Commission (LAC)- an independent recruitment agency - and appointed for a seven year term. The county manager is also manager for any town local authorities within the county.

Staffing

12. In all, at the end of 1995, there were just under 30,000 local authority staff made up of management, clerical/administrative, professional, technical, craft and general operative grades.

13. In addition to the county/city manager, some counties and cities have assistant managers. All counties have county secretaries and all the county and city authorities have finance officers. All of these posts are filled by open competition through the LAC.

14. The clerical/administrative structure consists of five grades. There is open competition at the entry grade and the next level. The basic qualification for all of these posts is second level education and recruitment is at local level. In general, all other clerical/administrative posts are filled through competitions confined to serving officers in the clerical administrative grades in local authorities, health boards, vocational education committees and certain other designated bodies (the 'common recruitment pool').

15. Parallel to the clerical/administrative structure, there is a wide range of grades dealing with specific services which are linked to the core grades for pay purposes. These include library grades, revenue collectors, storekeepers, legal assistants and many others.

16. The professional and technical structure is headed by the county/city engineer and generally the other engineering grades are senior executive engineer, executive engineer and assistant engineer. There is a range of analogous grades in other professional disciplines such as architects, planners, fire officers, chemists and many others. Recruitment to all of these grades is by open competition through the LAC. Technical grades include the draughtsman/ technician grades and clerk of works.

17. Apart from specific functions related to the appointment and suspension of managers, all functions related to staffing are executive functions of the manager. As indicated above, vacancies for senior management and professional posts are filled by public open competition, through the LAC. Vacancies for other local authority offices are filled directly by the local authority concerned in accordance with statutory regulations. Local authorities are also involved in sponsoring community employment schemes operated under the aegis of FÁS.

Local authority finance

18. Local authority financing is based on a combination of income sources both local and central. The main sources are:
    - rates on commercial and industrial buildings;
    - income from goods and services (charges, house loan repayments, housing rents, planning fees, etc);
    - Exchequer grants;
    - internal capital receipts (sale of houses, land etc); and
    - borrowing.

19. On current account, the total amount of local authority revenue in 1996 is estimated at IR£1,288 million made up of IR£757 million from local sources (rates, charges, etc) and IR£531 million from the Exchequer. Exchequer grants comprise both general grants, of which the rate support grant is the most significant, and specific grants such as for non-national roads and higher education student support. Current expenditure includes wages/salaries and other

administrative costs, insurance, debt servicing and payment of statutory demands to various bodies, housing maintenance and the cost of maintaining and operating capital facilities such as roads and water and waste water treatment plants.

20. On capital account, local authority projects, for which some IR£798 million is provided in the Public Capital Programme for 1996, include construction of local authority houses, road construction, provision of water and sewerage facilities, provision of fire, library and swimming pool facilities. These are mainly funded by one hundred per cent State grants, supplemented by local authorities' own capital receipts from various sources, including sales of houses to tenants, as well as borrowing for some purposes.

Sources of finance

21. The following tables indicate the sources of funding of current expenditure of local authorities as derived from the 1996 estimates prepared by them and the provision for local authorities under the 1996 Public Capital Programme:

Local Authority Finance (1996 estimate) - Current

Source	Total IR£m	%
Government Grants/Subsidies	531	41
Income from Goods and Services	418	33
Rates on Commercial/Industrial Property	339	26
Total	**1,288**	**100**

22. A summary of the provisions made in the 1996 Public Capital Programme for spending by local authorities is as follows:

Local Authority Finance (1996 PCP) - Capital

Item	Total IR£m
Housing	324.1
Roads*	315.8
Water & Sanitary Services	115.8
Environmental Services	16.3
Fire & Emergency Services	4.5
Miscellaneous	21.7
Total	**798.2**

IR£97.6 million of this amount is already included in the revenue figures in the previous table.

Regional authorities

23. Eight regional authorities were established in 1994, with a specific mandate to promote co-ordination of public services at the regional level; and to monitor and advise on the implementation of EU funding in the regions. The membership consists of county/city councillors from the region who are appointed by the constituent local authorities. They are supported by an operational committee which includes the relevant county and city managers and executives of various public agencies. Additionally, for EU purposes, a wide range of interests is represented on special monitoring committees. The regional authorities are funded by the constituent local authorities with special support provided by the Department of Finance in respect of EU related functions. The authorities operate at a modest level with current annual operating expenditure levels which range from about IR£100,000 to IR£200,000 and their staffing levels typically, include a Secretary and generally one or two other employees.

Eight
Regional Authority Areas
in Ireland

TABLE I

POPULATION, EXPENDITURE AND STAFFING OF EACH LOCAL AUTHORITY
Part I - County Councils

Local Authority	Population (1996 Preliminary Figures)	Current Expenditure (1996 estimate)▼ IR£	Staff at 31/12/95*
Carlow	41,616	11,191,704	235
Cavan	52,903	18,839,489	406
Clare	93,914	31,409,402	704
Cork	293,254	91,595,373	2,150
Donegal	129,435	41,238,050	838
Dun Laoghaire-Rathdown	189,836	52,382,200	1,247.5
Fingal	167,433	53,184,900	1,183.5
Galway	131,503	41,265,403	899
Kerry	125,863	41,338,000	919
Kildare	134,881	30,804,360	703.5
Kilkenny	75,155	24,272,600	580
Laois	52,798	24,704,317	362
Leitrim	25,032	13,587,180	271
Limerick	112,975	35,432,488	787
Longford	30,138	13,801,600	209
Louth	92,163	14,786,031	263
Mayo	111,395	37,442,324	906
Meath	109,371	29,455,395	478
Monaghan	51,266	16,281,500	296
Offaly	59,080	17,197,200	338
Roscommon	51,881	21,090,000	521
Sligo	55,645	15,703,150	357
South Dublin	218,401	57,800,700	1,167
Tipperary NR	57,944	17,519,581	451
Tipperary SR	75,364	23,232,994	488
Waterford	52,081	18,383,700	452
Westmeath	63,236	17,511,520	347
Wexford	104,314	27,202,100	561
Wicklow	102,417	27,294,044	555.5
Sub-total	**2,861,294**	**865,947,305**	**18,675**

* Staffing figures compiled from returns from local authorities to DOE.

▼ Expenditure figures are not adjusted for inter authority contributions.

TABLE I *Contd.*

Part II - County Boroughs

Local Authority	Population (1996 Preliminary Figures)	Current Expenditure (1996 estimate)▼ IR£	Staff at 31/12/95*
Cork	127,092	51,201,000	1,324
Dublin	480,996	245,548,731	6,345
Galway	57,095	16,382,700	295
Limerick	52,042	23,873,480	586
Waterford	42,516	15,157,711	294
Sub-total	**759,741**	**352,163,622**	**8,844**

* *Staffing figures compiled from returns from local authorities to DOE.*

▼ *Expenditure figures are not adjusted for inter authority contributions.*

TABLE I *Contd.*

Part III - Boroughs and Urban District Councils

Local Authority	Population (1996 Preliminary Figures)	Environs Population (1991)#	Current Expenditure (1996 estimate)▼ IR£	Staff at 31/12/95*
Arklow	8,448	-	1,991,251	42
Athlone	7,679	7,188	3,368,546	70
Athy	5,308	-	1,016,506	23
Ballina	6,842	1,604	1,649,330	34
Ballinasloe	5,629	99	1,624,040	37
Birr	3,352	776	858,557	19
Bray	25,207	1,857	4,789,736	81
Buncrana	3,310	1,270	966,871	17
Bundoran	1,704	-	759,290	12
Carlow	11,728	2,756	2,341,456	52
Carrickmacross	1,937	1,663	803,891	12
Carrick-On-Suir	5,174	-	1,178,107	25
Cashel	2,347	341	678,201	14
Castlebar	6,593	1,575	1,708,400	33
Castleblayney	1,879	909	412,522	13
Cavan	3,439	1,922	1,024,280	18
Clonakilty	2,714	236	762,960	8
Clones	1,906	253	474,363	11
Clonmel	15,119	1,031	4,596,963	92
Cobh	6,518	1,992	1,036,300	20
Drogheda	24,445	808	8,570,819	184
Dundalk	25,774	4,218	9,832,743	210
Dungarvan	7,169	-	1,686,755	41
Ennis	15,373	2,328	2,954,530	55
Enniscorthy	3,781	3,528	1,134,030	32
Fermoy	2,309	2,149	968,492	38
Kells	2,150	1,356	544,580	10
Kilkenny	8,494	9,154	3,411,935	92
Killarney	8,812	2,675	2,394,948	42

* *Staffing figures compiled from returns from local authorities to DOE.*

▼ *Expenditure figures are not adjusted for inter authority contributions.*

\# *Data from the 1996 census on the population figures of town environs are not yet available; environs data shown are from the 1991 census.*

TABLE I *Contd.*

Part III - Boroughs and Urban District Councils

Local Authority	Population (1996 Preliminary Figures)	Environs Population (1991)#	Current Expenditure (1996 estimate)▼ IR£	Staff at 31/12/95*
Kilrush	2,553	-	546,185	8
Kinsale	2,006	992	653,000	9
Letterkenny	7,254	3,540	2,087,307	47
Listowel	3,360	250	939,275	25
Longford	6,436	431	1,309,226	33
Macroom	2,456	-	705,704	13
Mallow	6,434	1,283	1,450,850	37
Midleton	3,263	2,961	835,015	17
Monaghan	5,609	196	1,693,415	46
Naas	14,071	-	1,840,730	32
Navan	3,440	8,291	1,241,399	23
Nenagh	5,631	300	1,229,192	28
New Ross	5,004	1,061	1,033,665	32
Skibbereen	1,923	-	419,015	8
Sligo	17,616	662	6,434,250	101
Templemore	2,117	137	362,300	9
Thurles	6,583	268	1,294,900	35
Tipperary	4,643	191	1,423,871	27
Tralee	19,027	637	5,187,450	108
Trim	1,782	2,401	505,850	12
Tullamore	9,213	808	1,963,431	45
Westport	4,249	-	1,183,225	27
Wexford	9,533	5,849	3,575,961	100
Wicklow	6,409	368	1,310,918	33
Youghal	5,626	296	1,114,008	25
Sub-total	**381,378**	**82,610**	**103,880,544**	**2,217**

* Staffing figures compiled from returns from local authorities to DOE.

▼ Expenditure figures are not adjusted for inter authority contributions.

\# Data from the 1996 census on the population figures of town environs are not yet available; environs data shown are from the 1991 census.

TABLE I *Contd.*

Part IV - Town Commissioners

Local Authority	Population (1996 Preliminary Figures)	Environs Population (1991)#	Current Expenditure (1996 estimate)▼ IR£	Staff at 31/12/95✠*
Ardee	3,443	335	28,520	0
Balbriggan	5,745	2,310	54,180	3
Ballybay	474	697	11,720	0
Ballyshannon	2,303	412	50,175	0
Bandon	1,703	3,005	15,855	0
Bantry	2,938	-	21,666	1
Belturbet	1,248	-	13,855	0
Boyle	1,688	502	17,460	1
Cootehill	1,459	339	18,629	1
Droichead Nua	11,778◆	291	83,250	1
Edenderry	3,596	217	20,300	0
Gorey	2,148	1,647	32,120	0
Granard	1,174	-	13,140	1
Greystones	9,649◆	1,129	44,450	0
Kilkee	1,330	-	25,300	1
Leixlip	13,194◆	-	83,160	1
Lismore	729	380	5,580	2
Loughrea	3,335	-	34,100	0
Mountmellick	2,320	508	13,211	0
Muinebheag	2,552	127	17,255	3
Mullingar	8,056	3,864	39,744	2
Passage West	3,629	196	13,580	0
Portlaoise	3,520	4,742	31,385	0
Shannon	7,920◆	-	58,600	0
Tramore	6,064◆	-	24,100	1
Tuam	3,483	2,092	50,390	1
Sub-total	**105,478**	**22,793**	**821,725**	**19**

* Staffing figures compiled from returns from local authorities to DOE.

✠ All towns have a town clerk, in some cases a county council officer assigned the duties on a part time basis. In these cases, the staff numbers are included in the county council figures in part 1 of this table.

▼ Expenditure figures are not adjusted for inter authority contributions.

Data from the 1996 census on the population figures of town environs are not yet available; environs data shown are from the 1991 census.

◆ The figures shown for these town commissioners are for 1991 as complete data from the 1996 census for such authorities are not yet available.

TABLE I *Contd.*

	Total Population(1996 Preliminary Figures)	Current Expenditure ▼ (1996 estimate) IR£	Staff at 31/12/95 *
County Councils	2,861,294 ▣	865,947,305 ▼	18,675
County Boroughs	759,741	352,163,622 ▼	8,844
Boroughs & UDCs	▣	103,880,544 ▼	2,217
Town Commissioners	▣	821,725 ▼	19
Grand Total	**3,621,035**	**1,322,813,196 ▼**	**29,755**

* *Staffing figures compiled from returns from local authorities to DOE.*

▼ *Expenditure figures are not adjusted for inter authority contributions of about IR£34m.*

▣ *County council population figures are inclusive of boroughs, urban district councils and town commissions for which complete 1996 figures are not yet available.*

TABLE II

LOCAL AUTHORITY RENTED HOUSES AT 31 DECEMBER, 1995

Local Authority	Number of dwellings occupied◆	Local Authority	Number of dwellings occupied◆
County Councils		**County Boroughs**	
Carlow	567	Cork	7,537
Cavan	721	Dublin	31,150
Clare	811	Galway	1,378
Cork	2,742	Limerick	3,231
Donegal*	2,669	Waterford*	2,349
Dun Laoghaire-Rathdown	3,616	**Sub-total**	**45,645**
Fingal	1,725		
Galway	1,731	**Boroughs & Urban District Councils**	
Kerry	2,191	Arklow	360
Kildare	1,377	Athlone*	251
Kilkenny	1,224	Athy	185
Laois	973	Ballina*	323
Leitrim*	668	Ballinasloe	274
Limerick	1,291	Birr*	153
Longford	735	Bray	916
Louth	437	Buncrana*	46
Mayo	1,391	Bundoran	36
Meath	1,258	Carlow	429
Monaghan	387	Carrickmacross	89
Offaly	671	Carrick-on-Suir	359
Roscommon	662	Cashel	137
Sligo*	586	Castlebar*	115
South Dublin*	2,868	Castleblayney	87
Tipperary NR	797	Cavan	290
Tipperary SR	1,000	Clonakilty	61
Waterford	665	Clones	55
Westmeath	668	Clonmel*	557
Wexford	1,375	Cobh*	205
Wicklow*	1,469	Drogheda	909
Sub-total	**37,275**	Dundalk	1,114

◆ *Housing figures compiled from returns from local authorities to DOE.*

* *1994 figures.*

Appendices

TABLE II *Contd.*

LOCAL AUTHORITY RENTED HOUSES AT 31 DECEMBER, 1995

Boroughs/Urban District Councils contd.	Number of dwellings occupied◆
Dungarvan*	358
Ennis	419
Enniscorthy*	279
Fermoy*	139
Kells	75
Kilkenny*	481
Killarney	196
Kilrush	133
Kinsale*	65
Letterkenny*	168
Listowel	148
Longford	290
Macroom*	82
Mallow	318
Midleton*	152
Monaghan	237
Naas	226
Navan	110
Nenagh	211
New Ross	405
Skibbereen	47
Sligo*	584
Templemore	99
Thurles*	253
Tipperary*	348
Tralee	932
Trim	56
Tullamore*	312
Westport*	94
Wexford	667
Wicklow	218
Youghal	240
Sub-total	**15,293**

Town Commissioners	Number of dwellings occupied◆
Ardee	1
Ballybay	3
Ballyshannon	10
Bandon*	7
Belturbet	5
Boyle	21
Cootehill	19
Droichead Nua*	32
Gorey*	2
Kilkee*	6
Loughrea	1
Mountmellick	2
Muinebheag	6
Mullingar*	6
Passage West*	6
Portlaoise*	7
Tuam	34
Sub-total	**168**
Grand Total	**98,381**

◆ *Housing figures compiled from returns from local authorities to DOE.*

* *1994 figures.*

Appendices

TABLE III

PUBLIC ROAD NETWORK IN 1995

County Council	National Primary# km	National Secondary# km	Non-National# km	Grand Total# km
Carlow	23	55	1,108	1,186
Cavan	65	61	2,877	3,003
Clare	57	180	3,935	4,172
Cork	237	259	11,514	12,010
Donegal	151	154	6,150	6,455
Dun Laoghaire-Rathdown	20	0	626	646
Fingal	48	0	985	1,033
Galway	153	277	6,152	6,582
Kerry	96	332	4,330	4,758
Kildare	112	30	2,090	2,232
Kilkenny	149	67	2,880	3,096
Laois	84	77	2,111	2,272
Leitrim	55	0	2,175	2,230
Limerick	138	53	3,344	3,535
Longford	41	55	1,464	1,560
Louth	74	49	1,167	1,290
Mayo	134	266	5,889	6,289
Meath	121	76	2,940	3,137
Monaghan	72	32	2,299	2,403
Offaly	18	122	1,845	1,985
Roscommon	102	144	3,690	3,936
Sligo	110	46	2,494	2,650
South Dublin	31	18	640	689
Tipperary NR	65	100	2,588	2,753
Tipperary SR	119	39	2,722	2,880
Waterford	69	36	2,427	2,532
Westmeath	97	83	1,923	2,103
Wexford	148	15	3,162	3,325
Wicklow	55	39	1,888	1,982
Sub-total	**2,644**	**2,665**	**87,415**	**92,724**

Roads figures compiled from returns from local authorities and NRA to DOE.

TABLE III *Contd.*

PUBLIC ROAD NETWORK IN 1995*

County Boroughs	National Primary# km	National Secondary# km	Non-National# km	Grand Total# km
Cork	19	3	327	349
Dublin	30	6	1,133	1,169
Galway	10	6	169	185
Limerick	15	2	156	173
Waterford	8	0	163	171
Sub-total	**82**	**17**	**1,948**	**2,047**
Grand Total km	**2,726**	**2,682**	**89,363**	**94,771***

Roads figures compiled from returns from local authorities and NRA to DOE.

* *In addition to the figure of 94,771 km there is a further 1,000 km approx. of local roads which are the responsibility of borough corporations and urban district councils.*

Appendix 3

Local development organisations and groups in each county recieving support under OPLURD and LEADER II Programme ◼

COUNTIES	CEBs*	PARTNERSHIPS	LEADER	COMMUNITY GROUPS
Carlow	Carlow CEB	Nil	Barrow-Nore-Suir Rural Development Ltd.	Ballon-Rathoe Development Group CANDO - Carlow Area Network Development Organisation
Cavan	Cavan CEB	County Cavan Partnership	Cavan-Monaghan Rural Development Co-op Soc. Ltd.	Nil
Clare	Clare CEB	Nil	Rural Resource Development Ltd.	Ennis West Partners OBAIR - (Newmarket-on-Fergus) West Clare Community Development Resource Centre Ltd.
Cork	Cork City CEB Cork County (N) CEB Cork County (S) CEB Cork County (W) CEB	Cork City	Ballyhoura Development Ltd. Blackwater Region LEADER Company East Cork Area Development Ltd. IRD Duhallow Ltd. West Cork LEADER Group	Avondhu Development Partnership Bantry Integrated Development Group East Cork Area Development Ltd. IRD Duhallow Ltd.
Donegal	Donegal CEB	Donegal Local Development Company Inishowen Partnership Board Pairtíocht Gaeltacht Thir Chonaill	Donegal Local Development Company Inishowen Community Group	Nil

◼ Data supplied by the Department of the Taoiseach.

* CEBs: County Enterprise Boards.

COUNTIES	CEBs*	PARTNERSHIPS	LEADER	COMMUNITY GROUPS
Dublin	Dublin City CEB Dun Laoghaire-Rathdown CEB Fingal CEB South Dublin CEB	Ballyfermot Partnership Ballymun Partnership Blanchardstown Area Partnership Bluebell/Rialto/Kilmainham/Inchicore Partnership Clondalkin Partnership Company Dublin Inner City Finglas Partnership KWCD Partnership Northside Partnership Southside Partnership Tallaght Partnership	Irish Country Holidays Rural Dublin LEADER Company Ltd.	Balbriggan Initiative Group Community Enterprise Society Ltd (Terenure) Lucan Community Council
Galway	Galway City/County CEB	Galway City Partnership Galway Rural Development Company Pairtíocht Chonamara	Comhdhail Oileaín na hÉireann Galway Rural Development Company	Nil
Kerry	Kerry CEB	Partnership Trá Lí South Kerry Partnership Ltd	Meitheal Forbartha na Gaeltachta Teo South Kerry Partnership Ltd Tuatha Chiarraí Ltd	Kerry Rural Development Sliabh Luachra Ltd Listowel Baronies Group Ltd Meitheal Forbarcha na Gaeltachta Teo
Kildare	Kildare CEB	North West Kildare/North Offaly Partnership	KELT - Kildare European LEADER II Teo	Action South Kildare Ltd
Kilkenny	Kilkenny CEB	Nil	Barrow-Nore-Suir Rural Development Ltd	Castlecomer District Community Development Network Kilkenny Community Action Network
Laois	Laois CEB	Nil	Laois Rural Development Company	Mountmellick Community Development Association Portlaoise Community Action Partnership Project
Leitrim	Leitrim CEB	Leitrim Partnership	Arigna Catchment Area Community Company	Nil

*   CEBs: County Enterprise Boards

COUNTIES	CEBs*	PARTNERSHIPS	LEADER	COMMUNITY GROUPS
Limerick	Limerick City CEB Limerick County CEB	Limerick West Limerick Resources Ltd	Ballyhoura Development Ltd Irish Farm Holidays Tipperary LEADER Group West Limerick Resources Ltd.	KHM Partnership
Longford	Longford CEB	Longford Community Resources Ltd	Longford Community Resources Ltd Association	Nil
Louth	Louth CEB	Drogheda Partnership Company Dundalk	Louth Rural Development Company	Nil
Mayo	Mayo CEB	North Mayo	Comhar Iorrais Teo South West Mayo Development Company Western Rural Development Company	Nil
Meath	Meath CEB	Nil	Meath Community Partnership Company	Navan Travellers Workshop Ltd North Meath Communities Development Association Trim Initiative for Development and Enterprise
Monaghan	Monaghan CEB	Monaghan Partnership Board	Cavan-Monaghan Rural Development Co-op Society Ltd	Nil
Offaly	Offaly CEB	North West Kildare/ North Offaly Partnership	Offaly LEADER II Company Ltd.	Tullamore Wider Options Group West Offaly Integrated Development Partnership
Roscommon	Roscommon CEB	Roscommon County Partnership	Arigna Catchment Community Company Mid-South Roscommon Rural Development Company	Nil
Sligo	Sligo CEB	County Sligo LEADER Partnership Company	Arigna Catchment Area Community Company Sligo County LEADER Partnership Company Ltd. Western Rural Development Company	Nil

* CEBs: County Enterprise Boards

COUNTIES	CEBs*	PARTNERSHIPS	LEADER	COMMUNITY GROUPS
Tipperary	Tipperary (NR) CEB Tipperary (SR) CEB	Nil	Barrow-Nore-Suir Rural Development Ltd Tipperary LEADER Group	Borrisokane Area Network District Clonmel Community Partnership Nenagh & District Community Network Roscrea Chamber of Commerce Enterprise Sub Committee
Waterford	Waterford City CEB Waterford County CEB	Waterford Waterford Area Partnership	Waterford Development Partnership Ltd.	Nil
Westmeath	Westmeath CEB	Westmeath Community Development Ltd.	Mid-South Roscommon Rural Development Company Westmeath Community Development Ltd.	Athlone Community Taskforce
Wexford	Wexford CEB	County Wexford Partnership Wexford Area Partnership	WORD - Wexford Organisation for Rural Development	Nil
Wicklow	Wicklow CEB	Bray Partnership	Wicklow Rural Partnership Ltd.	Arklow Community Enterprise Wicklow Working Together

*   CEBs: County Enterprise Boards

Agenda 21, New York: United Nations, (1992).

A Plan for Social Housing, Dublin: Department of the Environment, (1991).

Charting our Education Future, Dublin: Department of Education, (1995).

Devolution Commission, Interim Report, Dublin: Stationery Office, (1996).

Environmental Action Programme, Dublin: Department of the Environment, (1990).

Government Statement: Local Government Reform, Dublin: Government Information Services (4 July 1995).

Government Statement: Interim Report of Devolution Commission, Dublin: Government Information Services (1 August 1996).

KPMG Report - The Financing of Local Government in Ireland, Dublin: Stationery Office, (1996).

Local Agenda 21, Dublin: Department of the Environment, (1995).

Local Authority Reserved Functions - Recommendations of Working Group, Dublin: Department of the Environment, (1992).

National Road Safety Together Strategy, Dublin: Department of the Environment, (1996).

National Strategy for Traveller Accomodation, Dublin: Department of the Environment, (1996).

Operational Programme for Environmental Services (1994 - 1999), Dublin: Stationery Office, (1994).

Operational Programme for the Implementation of the EU LEADER II Initiative in Ireland (1994-1999), Dublin: Department of Agriculture (1996).

Operational Programme: Local Urban and Rural Development (1994 - 1999), Dublin: Stationery Office, (1995).

Operational Programme for Transport (1994 - 1999), Dublin: Stationery Office, (1994).

Operational Programme Urban - Ireland (1996 - 1999), Dublin: Department of the Taoiseach (1996).

Operational Strategy, Dublin: Department of the Environment, (1996).

Policy Agreement, A Government of Renewal, Dublin: (1994).

Programme for Competitiveness and Work, Dublin: Stationery Office, (1994).

Programme for Economic and Social Progress, Dublin: Stationery Office, (1991).

Recycling for Ireland, Dublin: Department of the Environment, (1994).

Report of Advisory Expert Committee on Local Government Reorganisation and Reform, Dublin: Stationery Office, (1991).

Report of Constitution Review Group, Dublin: Stationery Office, (1996).

Report of Reorganisation Commission - Towards Cohesive Local Government - Town and County, Dublin: Stationery Office, (1996).

Social Housing - The Way Ahead, Dublin: Department of the Environment, (1995).

Special Support Programme for Peace and Reconciliation in Northern Ireland and the Border Counties of Ireland, Dublin: Commission of European Community, (1995).

State of the Environment in Ireland, Dublin: EPA, (1996).

Telecommunications Antennae and Support Structures - Guidelines for Planning Authorities, Dublin: Stationery Office, (1996).

The Arts Plan, Dublin: The Arts Council, (1994).

Windfarm Development - Guidelines for Planning Authorities, Dublin: Stationery Office, (1996).

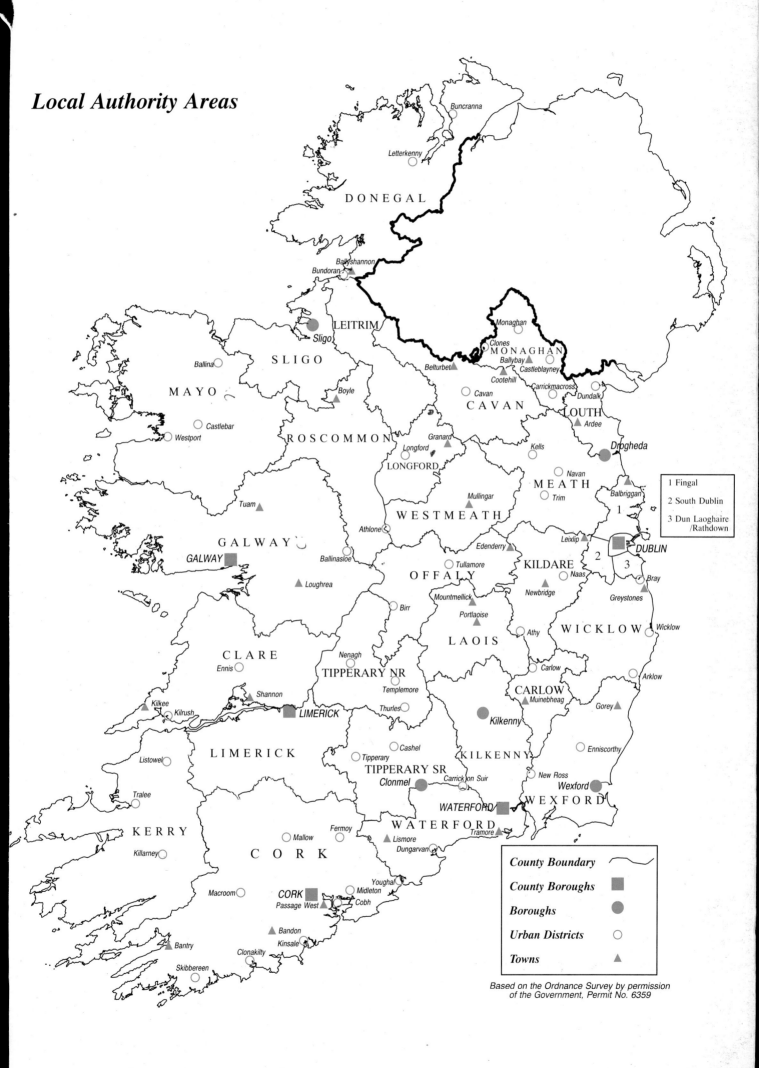

Local Authority Areas

1 Fingal
2 South Dublin
3 Dun Laoghaire
  /Rathdown

County Boundary
County Boroughs
Boroughs
Urban Districts
Towns

Based on the Ordnance Survey by permission
of the Government, Permit No. 6359